Saints of Derbyshire

Simon J Taylor &

Josephine Simister

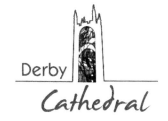

Derby
Cathedral

First published in 2021 by
Derby Cathedral Enterprises Ltd
18-19 Iron Gate, Derby DE1 3GP

British Library Cataloguing in Publication Data
A catalogue record for this book is available from the British Library
ISBN   978-1-7398357-0-5

9 781739 835705 >

Text designed and set in Sitka Banner by Josephine Simister.

Printed and bound by
John E Wright & Co Ltd
15-17 Brick St, Derby DE1 1DU

Contents

Contents

Foreword

From the Right Reverend Libby Lane, Bishop of Derby

I grew up in Derbyshire: it holds my heart.

As a child in Glossop, I enjoyed primary school, dance classes, Brownies and all the other normal things children do. When I was 11, a friend invited me to go to a tiny youth group that met at St John's Church in Charlesworth. As a child, I always liked to join in properly with things and so thought I ought to turn up at church as well. I turned up one Sunday morning on my own and was made to feel welcome - when I returned, they remembered my name. I was 'adopted' into the church family and their lives. They showed me every day faith, and encouraged me to get involved in everything from leading prayers to taking part in church governance. I will always be deeply grateful to God that those 'Derbyshire saints' loved me into faith.

Being Bishop of Derby has brought me home – an opportunity to return the love Derbyshire has given me. The episcopal ring I wear has Blue John running through it. It is uniquely Derbyshire and every time I put it on, it reminds me of the people and the places that formed me. I haven't had to grow to love Derbyshire and Derby because that love is already very deeply ingrained in me.

However, coming back to a place you think you know soon makes you realise that your experiences can be very different from those of other people, so it is a priority to get out and about to meet people in 'their' Derby and Derbyshire. There's still much of the county I have to explore. I want to hear people's stories, listen to their wisdom and find out about the things that matter to them. Over the coming years I will continue getting to know the people of Derbyshire and be known by them.

We are shaped by the connection we have with those around us. My own experience is that God's transformative work within me happens as God speaks to me through other people and through the spaces between us. The Bible talks about Christians being one body, fundamentally connected and mutually dependent. St Paul urges us to be committed to one another and to promote one another's growth to maturity of faith so that we build one another up in love (Ephesians 4:15-16).

That has been my experience of being part of the body of Christ in Derbyshire for significant parts of my life. I have learnt and grown in my faith from the people of this beautiful county. None of us is perfect, and I'm certainly aware of my own frailty and failures. But one way or another we rub the corners off one another as we participate together in God's work of refining and forming us. We are all influenced and impacted by the people around us and by those who have gone before us and so it shall ever be.

I hope that reading these stories of the saints of Derbyshire through history will have the same kind of impact upon you that knowing the people of Derbyshire today has had upon me. I pray that God will speak to you, comfort you, challenge and encourage you through their lives, examples and stories. Maybe they will inspire you to come and explore the places you read about and if so, then I hope and pray that you will find a warm welcome from today's saints in Derbyshire just as I did.

But above all, as you read about the lives of the Derbyshire saints portrayed so vividly and realistically in this compilation, I pray that you will see beyond their lives to the Christ they loved and served. As you learn about them, may you also learn from them and encounter this Jesus, who was at work in them, in your own life and situations too. That way you will join with the saints of Derbyshire (and indeed with all the saints throughout the world and across the centuries), knowing you are loved beyond measure by Christ and be inspired to loving without restraint in return, for His sake.

✝Libby Derby

Derby Diocese

Locations mentioned in the text

(see also Appendix Two)

Charlesworth

Grindleford ×

Eckington ×

Eyam ×

Tideswell ×

Chatsworth ×

×Chesterfield

×Wingerworth

Monyash ×

Birchover

Cratcliffe × ×   Matlock ×

Bonsall×   ×   Matlock Bath

×Dethick

Cromford×   ×Lea

Wirksworth×   ×Crich

South Normanton ×

×Fritchley

Ilam×   Ashbourne ×

Belper ×

Denby ×

Hulland Ward×   ×Milford

Mugginton×   ×Duffield

Rodsley×   ×

Kedleston

Longford×

Dale Abbey ×

Radbourne×   × ×Breadsall

Derby

Somersal Herbert ×

Findern

Egginton ×

Swarkestone ×

Newton Solney   ×

×Repton

Winshill   ×

×Ingleby

Trent Washlands   ×

×Bretby

× Breedon on the Hill

Burton ×   ×Stapenhill

List of Illustrations

Linocuts accompanying prayers

Sketches *from the authors' photographs, primary sources, and resources available in the public domain.*

Cover

All Saints and All Souls stained glass windows by Ceri Richards (photograph provided by Derby Cathedral), against a Derbyshire landscape near Hartington (photograph by Josephine Simister).

Introduction

The beauty of the county of Derbyshire is matched only by the fascinating lives of the people who have inhabited it over the centuries. This book will introduce you to over fifty people and their lives. You will find stories of love, passion, murder, miracles, sacrifice, innovation, exploration and downright stubbornness. They all have two things in common: a connection to Derbyshire and a claim to be a saint.

The connection to Derbyshire is simple to establish. We have chosen saints who have a deep connection to a place within the county of Derbyshire or the Diocese of Derby (the two are nearly, but not quite the same). We have also included only those who have died.

The claim to be a saint needs further explanation. The word 'saint' simply means 'holy one'. Some of those included in this book have been formally declared to be Saints, but most have not. The Bible says that we are 'surrounded by so great a cloud of witnesses' (Hebrews 12.1), and it is their witness to God that has helped us to choose these Derbyshire saints. This has given us a very broad cast of characters, so broad that you will find a number of points of disagreement between the saints. This too is part of their witness.

Our hope is that this book will connect you to the saints, and through them to Derbyshire, to the history of the times in which they lived, and to God. Each story refers to places and items that you could go and see, and each contains a prayer of thankfulness for the lives of the saints described. We have included a 'Where to go' section that provides directions and an 'Also interesting' section that adds diverse information related to the main story. We have gathered the places that are referred to in Appendix Two. For those who may want to celebrate a saint on a special day, we have gathered those days (although many are our own suggestions), in Appendix One.

We have been intrigued and delighted by our discovery of the different saints of Derbyshire. We rejoice in sharing this selection with you and look forward to learning of new saints and new stories. This is a book designed to be taken on picnics, rambles and journeys around the county. Besides being inspired by the beauty of Derbyshire, we hope that you will also enjoy treading the same ground that these extraordinary characters trod before and exploring new places that are associated with them. We are sure that you will find laughter and poignancy and come away enriched by these connections.

Simon J. Taylor
Josephine Simister
Michaelmas 2021

01: The A, B, C (and D) of Christianity's Arrival:

Adda, Betti, Cedd and Diuma

Wirksworth, 7ᵗʰ century

The stories of the saints of Derbyshire begin in the year 653AD. with marriage, kings and a side-track.

Fragment of Anglo-Saxon carving in stone, from St Mary's Church, Wirksworth

In the 7ᵗʰ century, England was divided into a number of small kingdoms with different belief systems. As their kings struggled for land and supremacy, alliances were struck through marriages.

Peada, sub-king of the Middle Angles (roughly Leicestershire and Northamptonshire) wanted to marry Alchflaed, the daughter of Oswy, king of Northumbria. This was complicated because Oswy was a Christian and Peada was not. A deal was struck: the marriage could go ahead if Peada became a Christian. Peada eagerly agreed and was instructed in the Christian faith. He was baptised along with his soldiers, earls and household, by Bishop Finan of Lindisfarne at King Oswy's estate on Hadrian's Wall. He then married Alchflaed.

Peada baptised by Bishop Finan of Lindisfarne: detail from a window in St Wystan's Church, Repton

Peada returned home to Repton, the capital of his father Penda's kingdom of Mercia, with four priests who were instructed to teach Christianity to his people. These four were Adda, Betti, Cedd and Diuma, chosen, according to the Venerable Bede, 'for their learning and holy life'.

On their way from Northumbria to Repton, the four may well have passed through Wirksworth on the old Roman roads that were still in use. Wirksworth was part of the kingdom of Mercia, and it has a claim to be the second Christian foundation in Derbyshire after Repton. Built around lead mining and quarrying, Wirksworth is still a significant market town in Derbyshire.

We know varying amounts about the four priests, who were all monks and priests of the Celtic tradition, which had origins in Ireland

and was distinct from the Catholic tradition centred on Rome. These monks valued praying, reading the Bible, and caring for the poor and needy. That is how they taught people about Christianity: by embodying it and living it out. They would preach and talk as well, but their teaching was of a piece with the way they lived.

Celtic monks respected kings, and were often used as emissaries. But there was a strong tradition of standing up to kings when necessary. Adda, Betti, Cedd and Diuma all came out of this way of life.

What we know specifically about the four is as follows:

Adda was the brother of Utta, the Abbot of Gateshead.

Cedd was the leader of the group. One of four brothers, he was brought up on Lindisfarne by St Aidan (who brought Christianity to northern England from Iona). A gifted linguist, he acted as translator at the Council of Whitby which reconciled the Celtic and Roman churches. He went as a missionary to the East Saxons, where he had notable success and was ordained Bishop, and founded many churches and monasteries in what is now Essex. Cedd died in 664, back in Northumbria.

Diuma was an Irishman and we shall encounter him again, as the Bishop of Mercia at Repton (Chapter 2).

Of **Betti** we know almost nothing from the written sources. However, there is a story that tells that Betti founded the first church in Wirksworth.

A Prayer for Pilgrims

God of all our journeys,

    we give you thanks for Adda, Betti, Cedd and Diuma,

    for their service to the poor

    and for their bringing of Good News.

May we follow in the way of Christ,

    serving those we encounter,

    and being good news to all whom we meet.

We pray for all who travel,

    that they might know your travelling mercies,

    and arrive with joy at their destination.

We ask this in the name of Jesus,

    who came to serve and to bring your love to this world.

    Amen.

The mission to Mercia: detail from the Wirksworth Stone

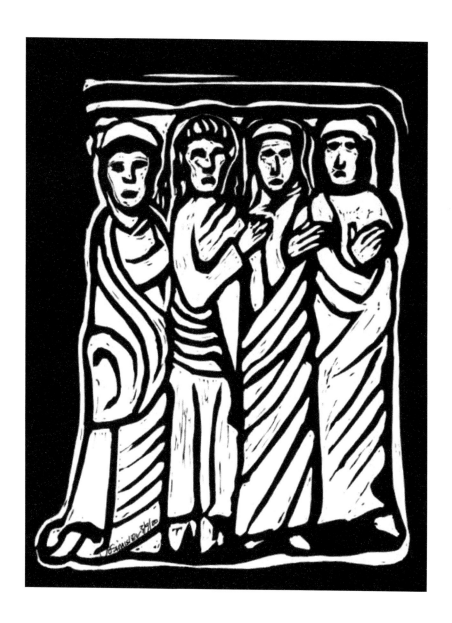

Where to go

St Mary's Church, St Mary's Gate, Wirksworth, Matlock DE4 4DQ

Wirksworth stands at the head of the Ecclesbourne valley and is on bus routes between Derby and Bakewell, and Ashbourne and Matlock.

The church may in fact mark the source of the Ecclesbourne stream. It certainly appears to have given a name to the valley, 'eccles' meaning 'church' or a place of Christian worship.

The present church is set in a grassy precinct and mostly dates from the 13th century. Some beautiful and unique Anglo-Saxon carvings are preserved among the stones of its walls. Its great treasure, the 'Wirksworth Stone', is displayed on the north wall and shows the highest stonemasons' art achievable at the time it was made, which tells us that Wirksworth must have become a very important centre of Christianity and that someone highly cherished was being buried there. See the section following ('Also interesting') for a fuller explanation of its carvings, and also of the origins of another carving known as T'Owd Man.

The 'King and Queen' can be found just inside the church, to the right of the main entrance. Dating back about 1300 years, the panel appears to have been randomly placed in the walls during the rebuilding of the church during the thirteenth century. The precise age and origins are not known.

Also interesting

T'Owd Man:

T'Owd Man, a Saxon carving in stone, from St Mary's Church, Wirksworth

The Old Man is a little figure of a lead miner with his pick and kibble (basket). It is not known why T'Owd Man was created or who his creators were. Some scholars think he could be a mythic representation of the so-called 'guardian spirit' of ancient lead mines who dwelt deep in the shafts and caverns watching over the early miners in their highly-dangerous work. Lead mining was a key industry in the area from at least Roman times, and Wirksworth was the centre for the trade.

He is presently to be found embedded in the west wall of the south transept inside St Mary's Church, but is believed to have come originally from a church in Bonsall which was being rebuilt – and indeed, it is probable he had already been used elsewhere before that.

Along with some other interesting fragments, he was rescued for safekeeping but left behind when the other pieces were restored to the Bonsall church. He found his way to St Mary's and was placed in the wall during the 19th century restoration which also uncovered the Wirksworth Stone.

·The·Wirksworth·Stone··

The Wirksworth Stone:

This intricately carved coffin lid hangs on the north wall of St Mary's Church. It dates from between 700 and 800 AD. and is carved in the Northumbrian style. It was rediscovered in 1820 underneath the pavement in front of the altar.

As noted previously, the stone and the site of its burial suggest a significant person was buried there. It is tempting, and not unreasonable, to suggest that this was the grave of the founder of the church, Betti, the monk and priest from Northumberland who brought Christianity to Wirksworth and to Derbyshire.

The Stone has eight scenes, telling stories from the life of Jesus and of his mother Mary. On the left-hand side, the Stone tells of Jesus. The four panels show the washing of the disciples' feet, the crucifixion, the descent to hell and the ascension.

Mary's life is told through the angel announcing she will have a child, taking Jesus to the Temple as a child, and her death. A final panel shows Mary and Jesus sending the church into the whole world.

The stories all reinforce one another to tell of service and being sent to bring the good news of Christianity to everyone. Can you find the figures shown in the image accompanying the prayer?

If the coffin lid is Betti's, it is a fitting memorial for the monk who in service and preaching brought Christianity to Derbyshire and to Wirksworth.

Clypping the church:

On the 8th September (or the following Sunday), there is a ceremony of 'Clypping the church' in which the church building is encircled as a way of embracing and giving thanks for it, and praying for the continuance of God's presence through the present and into the future.

02: Royalty, Geese and Murder: Seven Repton Saints:

Diuma, Ermenilda, Werburgh, Aelfritha, Edburga, Guthlac and Wystan

Repton, 7th-9th centuries

The village of Repton in south Derbyshire was once the capital of the kingdom of Mercia. After Peada's conversion and the arrival of Christianity, Repton became a centre of faith to match its political importance. However, the mixture of faith and politics was not always an easy one, and so the stories of the Repton saints include holiness and murder.

Diuma

Of the four who brought Christianity to Repton, Cedd was soon recalled to Northumberland and to a new mission. Betti probably went to found a church in Wirksworth, as we have seen. Adda appears to vanish from the record. It was Diuma who carried on the work of organising and establishing a church and the teaching, pastoral work and care for the poor that went with this. Diuma was the only one of the four sent from Northumbria whose roots were outside Britain. An Irishman, he became the bishop of the Mercians and Middle Angles, together with the people of Lindsey in Lincolnshire. Across this huge area, he worked tirelessly to teach and proclaim the faith. At Repton, he seems to have established a double monastery (for both men and women) and built the first church. Eventually Diuma died and the Venerable Bede records that, 'Diuma converted many to the Faith, and died among the Middle Angles in the district known as In-Feppingum'. The success of Diuma's work of establishing Christianity in Mercia is marked by his burial amongst the people he came to know, serve and love. There is still a Bishop of Repton, but Diuma was the first.

Ermenilda (or Eormenhild)

Diuma's work had firmly established Christianity in Mercia, and especially in the royal family. The next Repton saint is one of a number of royal women saints. Ermenilda was the daughter of King Eorcenberht of Kent and St Seaxburh of Ely. She married King Wulfhere of Mercia, and this is her connection to Repton.

After Wulfhere's death in 675 she became a nun and then abbess of Minster-in-Sheppey and Ely. After her death and burial in Ely, she was revered as a saint. She was known for her protection of children. One tale tells that some schoolboys, fearing the monk who was their school master, went to her tomb and prayed for her help. The monk found them there and took them away and beat them, scorning their prayers to Ermenilda. That night, as he lay in bed, the master was visited by Ermenilda. She bound the feet that had run to the shrine to remove the boys, and the hands that had beaten them. He was in agony and could not move. In the morning, he summoned the boys and begged them to forgive him and to carry him back to the saint's tomb and pray for his healing. This they did and he walked home again, a changed man.

Ermenilda represents an important tradition of royal women becoming nuns, then abbesses and then being venerated as saints.

Some of this is undoubtedly down to their royal connections, kings taking some delight from the prestige of being related to saints. But this cannot wholly explain the way that royal saints were venerated. They gave up riches and social standing to live under obedience, and the care with which they served the communities around them must also be part of the holiness that is recognised in this way.

Werburgh (or Werbergh or Werberga)

Werburgh was the daughter of King Wulfhere and Ermenilda and was born in Stone, Staffordshire. She was educated by St Chad (who moved the seat of the Bishop of the Mercians from Repton to Lichfield). Werburgh became a nun at Ely, where she was tutored by her great-aunt Etheldreda, the first abbess of Ely and a former queen of Northumbria.

The seclusion of a convent provided a safe place for royal children, a refuge from the ongoing plotting and warfare that was a feature of this time. As a nun, Werburgh developed a reputation for humility. But her status as a member of the royal family was not something that Werburgh lost. She was asked by King Ethelred, her uncle and her father's successor as King of Mercia, to oversee all the monasteries in Mercia.

Werburgh took this task very seriously, reforming existing monasteries and establishing new ones. She was much loved by those in her care and developed the reputation for knowing the secrets of people's hearts and having a gift of prophecy. A number of miracles were attributed to Werburgh, but the most famous concerns geese.

On one occasion a flock of geese were troubling a farm at Weedon, near Chester. Werburgh commanded the geese to go into a barn, where they stayed for the night. In the morning, she ordered them to leave. They refused, as the farmer had caught, cooked and eaten one of the geese the night before. Werburgh asked for the remains of the goose to be brought to her and prayed that it be restored to life. The goose was restored to wholeness and to life, after which the whole flock of geese left and never returned. Because of this story, Werburgh is often depicted with a goose.

Repton records Werburgh as the first Abbess of Repton. Later she succeeded her great aunt as Abbess of Ely. She died on 3rd February, 699 at Trentham and was buried at Hanbury (her remains were later translated to Chester: she is that city's patron).

Aelfritha

Of Aelfritha, less is known. She was abbess of Repton, succeeding Werburgh. In 697 she received Guthlac into the monastery at Repton.

Guthlac is received into the monastery by Aelfritha, as shown in a panel from the stained glass window in St Wystan's Church.

Edburga (also written as Ecgburh or Eadburh)

Edburga was daughter of King Aldwulf of East Anglia. King Wulfhere invited her to become abbess of Repton to succeed Aelfritha. This may have been due to her family relationship to Queen Ermenilda, who was her second cousin. She died around 700 and a pilgrim's guide from about 300 years later records that Edburga 'resteth ... in the Minster of Southwell, near the water of the Trent'. Whether this was her original burial place or her remains were moved there later is unclear. Her relics were certainly venerated in Southwell throughout the Middle Ages.

Edburga features in the life of Guthlac because she sent him a lead coffin and a fine linen sheet in which Guthlac was buried. Guthlac died later than Edburga, which has led to puzzlement in some quarters. It seems to us that Edburga's gift was sent long before Guthlac died. Coffins and linen were substantial gifts, and would have been kept until needed. This may be a particular gift of prophecy, but it is certainly a gift of great generosity on Edburga's part.

Guthlac

Guthlac has already entered our story. He was a prince of Mercia, and as a young man he fought in the king's army. His biographer, Felix, records that, 'he collected a great troop and host of his companions and equals, and himself took weapons. Then wreaked he his grudges on his enemies, and burned their city, and ravaged their towns, and widely through the land he made much slaughter'.

Guthlac led this campaign of barely restrained violence for about nine years, until at the age of 24 he saw a vision of his death. Moved to repent, he swore that if God would spare him through the night, he would serve him for the rest of his life. In the morning, he made the sign of the cross, said goodbye to his men, and went to Repton where he was received into the monastery by Aelfritha.

In Repton, Guthlac learned the monastic disciplines of fasting and prayer. In particular, he learned the Psalms by heart. These ancient Biblical prayers continue to be the foundation of all Christian prayer.

After two years at Repton, Guthlac left to become a hermit at Crowland in Lincolnshire. There he put to use all that he had learned in the monastery at Repton.

Aided by the Apostle Bartholomew, on whose feast day he arrived at Crowland, we are told he fought demons and lived a simple life of prayer. Guthlac was able to understand the speech of the strange British-speaking demons because as a child he had spent time in exile among native Britons.

In Crowland, Guthlac became at peace with himself and with the natural world. Stories tell of how he could command the ravens, and how sparrows would sit on him and sing. Many people came to visit him in his hermitage, and there are many stories of his miracles of healing.

Amongst his visitors was another noble warrior, Hwaetred, who fell into rages in which he inflicted damage on himself and on others. He had killed three men with an axe in one of these furies. Perhaps recognising a kindred spirit, Guthlac took him into church and with prayer managed to break the power of the demon. Hwaetred was healed and at peace.

Guthlac was a counsellor of kings, bishops, abbots and exiles. His gift for prophecy lasted even after his death. When King Athelbald came to pray at Guthlac's tomb, Guthlac appeared to him and prophesied about his future kingdom.

Guthlac died after 15 years living as a hermit. He was taken ill when praying on the Wednesday before Easter. Knowing he was dying, he sang mass and preached the Gospel on Easter Day. Before he died he asked that his sister Pega, a hermit at nearby Peachurch, should bury him in the coffin that Edburga had sent him. As Guthlac died, on the Wednesday after Easter, there was a great brightness that surrounded the hermitage, and the songs of angels could be heard. A year after his burial, he was exhumed and his body was found to be uncorrupted, a sign of his sanctity (as understood at that time).

Wystan (or Wigstan)

The final Repton saint of this period is another noble warrior, Wystan (or Wigstan). His father Wiglaf declined the kingship of Mercia, preferring a life in the monastery. That left Wystan's great uncle Beorhtfrith as King.

Beorhtfrith feared that Wystan might challenge him for the throne, or that others might use Wystan to do so. And so Beorhtfrith murdered Wystan on the eve of Pentecost in 840, and Wystan was buried in the crypt of the church that now bears his name in Repton. A column of light shot up to heaven from the place where Wystan was murdered and remained visible for thirty days. This was taken as a sign of his innocence and his martyrdom.

His shrine at Repton became a place of miracles and pilgrimage. Later, King Cnut removed Wystan's relics to Evesham.

A statue of Wystan stands over the entrance to St Wystan's Church in Repton

Guthlac and Wystan show different ways in which the church in 8th and 9th century England responded to the violence in politics and society.

In Guthlac, we see the conversion of one who was part of the problem. A thug, bully and arrogant leader of an army, Guthlac renounces all of this to follow the way of God. Having renounced violence, Guthlac became someone who could help others afflicted with this plague. His healing of Hwaetred shows his compassion in helping others to turn away from violence and follow the way of Jesus.

Converting people one at a time is very effective, but it is a slow approach to removing violence from society. However, the church had other methods, as the story of Wystan shows.

Wystan was the victim of political assassination, and not the only one at this time (as we shall see in chapter 4). In declaring him a saint and making his tomb a place of pilgrimage, the church was effective in condemning the political violence and weakening the position of those who sought to gain or consolidate power in this way.

Both are important ways in which the church witnessed to the Prince of Peace, and to the reconciliation that is at the heart of the Christian faith.

A Prayer for Pilgrims

Jesus, Prince of Peace,

we give you thanks for Diuma, Ermenilda, Werburgh,

Aelfritha, Edburga, Guthlac and Wystan,

for their witness to your life and to peace,

for the way in which they built and nurtured communities,

and for their courage, compassion and care.

May we follow in the way of Christ,

serving and building up our communities,

and working for peace in this world.

We pray for our nation and our communities,

that they may be places of care and nurture

and know the peace that comes from justice.

We ask this in your name,

whose death brought reconciliation to the whole world.

Amen.

'Holy air encased in stone': the Crypt at Repton

Where to go

Go to the village of Repton, where you can find a Repton Trail which is helpful and informative.

Spend a good amount of time in St Wystan's Church, DE65 6FH. The church has many of the Repton saints depicted in its windows, stonework and artwork (look hard for Aelfritha, who can be seen in a window behind the modern kitchen unit).

The 8th century crypt became a shrine to Wystan. Concealed at a later date, this has preserved it wonderfully and it was rediscovered in the 18th century.

A beautiful 'tree of life' candle stand enables pilgrims today to pray in this place, which Sir John Betjeman described as 'holy air encased in stone'.

Also interesting

The Guthlac Roll:

The British Library has released the fully digitised Guthlac Roll (Harley Roll Y6), a manuscript containing exquisite illustrations of his story, see https://blogs.bl.uk/digitisedmanuscripts/2014/04/on-a-roll.html.

The roll in its present state opens with half of a roundel that illustrates the sleepless night on which the young Guthlac, surrounded by his slumbering fellow-soldiers, resolved to devote himself to a life of religion. It includes scenes with his sister Pega, King Aethelbald listening intently to his advice, and a tender scene of his burial.

Viking mass grave in the Vicarage Garden:

The centuries following the stories in this chapter are full of invasion and slaughter, as the Vikings settled the land and over-wintered their army around Repton.

The excavations of a mass grave found where the monastery once stood (now within the vicarage garden) are regularly discussed in television documentaries. Here is some of the detail: https://www.archaeology.co.uk/articles/resolving-repton.htm.

Excavations in the 1970s and 1980s confirmed that a significant company of Vikings had overwintered at Repton, as mentioned in the Anglo-Saxon Chronicle, but subsequently it was realised that the site was not large enough for the entire Great Army. Extensive excavations uncovered a large defensive ditch abutting the church, revealing a ditch of a distinctive D-shape that is reminiscent of fortifications in Scandinavian towns of the period, albeit on a smaller scale.

A number of burials with distinctly Scandinavian grave goods were discovered, both within and outside the enclosure, including one that included five coins dating to AD 872-875.

A double grave of two men puzzled the archaeologists for a time, but DNA has now shown these are almost certainly a father and son of high status. Their burial place was in a prominent location with the remains of a stone cross shaft over it.

West of the church, in the vicarage garden, the jumbled remains of at least 264 people were excavated from a shallow mound over a partially destroyed Anglo-Saxon building. These are thought to be the 9th century battle dead of the Viking Great Army. They were mostly men, and aged 18-45 at the time of their deaths – about one-fifth were women.

Further significant finds of gaming pieces and lead weights downriver towards Foremark and further afield at Torksey in Lincolnshire point to Viking camps at points suitable for a safe harbour. Foremark is only a few hundred metres from Heath Wood, home to at least 60 Scandinavian burial mounds representing the only largescale Viking Age cremation cemetery known in England.

Viking presence is supported in local place names with Old Norse elements – Torksey, Foremark, Ingleby, Bretby, Swarkestone – and clearly there is much more to be discovered.

03: Storms, Swans and Solitude:

Modwen and Hardulph

Stapenhill and Ingleby, 7ᵗʰ century

Modwen

Modwen (or Modwenna) was an Irish noble woman who came to Derbyshire as a pilgrim on her way to Rome. With her companions Lazar and Althia, she founded an abbey on an island in the middle of the River Trent. She called this island St Andrew's Island or Andressey after the abbey. It is very near to what is now called Burton-on-Trent. Modwen used the local water to heal disease. It is claimed she even cured the prince who was later to become King Alfred the Great.

The island of Andressey and St Modwen's Church, with Andressey Bridge over the River Trent

Later the Abbey was moved into Burton, and the monks found the local water to be excellent for brewing, so Modwen may be credited as foundress of Burton's brewery industries! Today a church dedicated to St Modwen stands on the site of Burton Abbey. Modwen became abbess and stayed for seven years, before continuing her pilgrimage to Rome.

On her return from Rome, Modwen founded another church nearby, at what is now Stapenhill. While in Rome she had met the Pope, the successor of St Peter, so she dedicated the new church to St Peter. A church still stands on that site today.

Later, Modwen went to Scotland as a missionary and died in Langfortin, near Dundee, at the incredible age of one hundred and thirty. At her death, her companions saw her soul taken to heaven by silver swans. Her body and her pilgrim staff were returned to Burton for burial, originally at Andressey and later in Burton Abbey.

Many miracles are associated with Modwen. A pagan girl who learned about Jesus and became a Christian had died suddenly, before she could be baptised. Modwen prayed beside her deathbed, in tears and crying out to God. God restored the girl to life and Modwen had her baptised immediately. The girl went on to live a full life and became a nun in Modwen's abbey.

After her death, Modwen's reputation as a miracle worker continued to grow. By the fifteenth century, an image of Modwen with her staff and a red cow was very popular in Burton as a help to women suffering with labour pains.

Hardulph (or Hardulf)

Also on the borders of Derbyshire, but further along the River Trent, a hermit called Hardulph was living. Little is known about him, except that his hermitage was at Ingleby in Derbyshire, and he is buried nearby at Breedon in Leicestershire. Sometimes he is known as 'the Hermit of Breedon'.

Hardulph and Modwen knew one another. Hardulph would often visit Modwen, a short trip along the River Trent. They would read the lives of the saints together. On one occasion, Hardulph forgot to bring the book, so Modwen despatched two of her nuns to go and fetch it from Hardulph's hermitage.

The nuns rowed along the river but were caught up in a storm. At a place called Leigh their boat overturned and sank to the bottom of the river, trapping them beneath.

Meanwhile, Modwen and Hardulph began to wonder where the nuns had gone. Modwen realised that they had been sent out in a storm and feared for their safety. Hardulph was less concerned and urged Modwen to join him in praying for the pair.

At the end of their prayers, a dry path had opened up in the river. Hardulph and Modwen were able to walk on the dry riverbed to Leigh and find the boat.

Modwen lifted the boat up, discovering it to be light as a feather, and found the two girls hidden underneath it. Once all four had got into the boat, now the right way up, the water came back into the river, and all were carried home.

A 9th century frieze of pilgrims in St Hardulph's church, Breedon

Both Modwen and Hardulph suffer from being confused with other people. Modwen has been associated with the Irish saint Monenna, who lived at the time of St Patrick in the late 5th century. Hardulph is associated with Eardwulf, the 8th-9th century king of Northumbria who ordered Alkmund's assassination (see chapter 4). It is hard to disentangle their lives, but if Modwen and Hardulph did meet and talk together about the lives of the saints, then they cannot be the same people as Monenna and Eardwulf.

Modwen shows us the freedom that noble women had to travel, and her clear authority as an abbess and a founder and patron of churches. Her life was a long pilgrimage, with lengthy stops along the way. She moved from Ireland to Burton to Rome to Burton to

Scotland, at all times seeking to follow Jesus and to help those she met.

She and Hardulph were both committed to a life of solitude and silence, in which they could learn to pray and encounter God. It was their prayers and their closeness to God which led to so many stories of miracles being told about them.

A Prayer for Pilgrims

God of silence and of storm,

we give you thanks for Modwen and for Hardulph,

for their trust in the power of prayer,

for the silence in which they lived,

and for the life that they brought to those around them.

May we follow in the way of Christ

finding your presence in the midst of storms

and lifting burdens from the lives of others.

We pray for all who travel by water,

that they might know your protection

and your presence in calm and in storm.

We ask this in the name of Jesus

who calmed a storm and walked on the sea.

Amen.

The upturned coracle in the River Trent in full flood

Where to go

Modwen

Churches still stand on the sites of two places with which Modwen has close association, and the site of her abbey is in the Trent Washlands sculpture park, along with a statue.

St Modwen's, Burton:

Burton Abbey, where Modwen's remains were buried and a shrine to Modwen once stood, is now St Modwen's parish church, DE14 1HA. The church stands on the Market Place.

St Peter's, Stapenhill:

A church with the papal dedication to St Peter still stands in Stapenhill on the site of the church that Modwen founded. The church is on Stapenhill Road, DE15 9AF.

The Trent Washlands:

A walk from Stapenhill to Burton leads across the Trent Washlands, a public park on the flood plain, maintained by the National Forest. A sculpture trail through the Washlands includes a statue of Modwen, looking rather like an alien. The site of her abbey is in the nearby woods, though the abbey itself was destroyed in Viking raids – another sculpture represents the prow of a Viking ship. There is also a sculpture of a Marmite jar, which is perhaps the best of the public art in the park. For those not walking, there is an entrance at Meadowside Drive, DE14 1TL.

Hardulph

The Anchor Church:

Hardulph's hermitage is a cave at the Anchor Church, between the villages of Ingleby and Foremark, at DE65 6EJ.

From Ingleby, on the edge of the village, a signpost points to the Anchor Church. From there, it is a short walk along the muddy riverside path to the caves. The path goes on to emerge just outside Foremark.

The Anchor Church by the River Trent at Ingleby

The Anchor Church, now sporting a range of graffiti, has been used by less saintly people since Hardulph.

In the 12th century, it was used by a monk named Bernard, who lived there as penance for his part in deceiving Hugo de Burdett and his wife Johanne. This was part of a plot by the Baron of Boyville who wanted Johanne for himself. He bribed Bernard to convince Hugo to go on crusade to the Holy Land. There he was betrayed to the Saracens, and told that his wife had been unfaithful. Meanwhile Baron Boyville told Johanne that Hugo was dead and forced her to marry him. However, Bernard wanted more money, and when the Baron did not pay, he sprung Hugo from captivity and told him that his wife was being unfaithful with another man. Hugo returned home, killed the Baron and severed his wife's hand on which was her wedding ring. Much later, Bernard, now a penitent at the Anchor Church, died. But first he sent for Hugo, and gave him a parchment with an account of the whole sorry affair. There is tragedy and misogyny in equal measure in this story.

A later 17th century entry in the parish Registers of Repton speaks of 'Ye foole at Anchor Church'. In the 18th century the landowner, Sir Robert Burdett, a descendant of Hugo, enlarged the cave to enable parties to take place there.

St Hardulph's Church, Breedon on the Hill (also known as the Priory Church of St Mary and St Hardulph):

St Hardulph's Church in Breedon on the Hill, Leicestershire, is named for Hardulph. It stands on the site of a 7th century monastery founded by the Mercian kings. The story of Hardulph and Modwen probably predates the monastery. Inside the church there are some stunning 9th century carvings, but nothing other than its dedication that speaks of Hardulph himself.

Leigh, where the boat capsized and was miraculously saved, is a name that is lost. It was presumably along the Trent between Ingleby and Burton.

A 9th century frieze of waterfowl in St Hardulph's church, Breedon

Also interesting

The River Trent and Swarkestone Causeway:

Leigh may be lost, but the area is still a notorious flood plain.

The River Trent is the third-longest river in the United Kingdom and is known for dramatic flooding after storms and spring snowmelt, which in past times often caused the river to change course. You can get an idea of the dangers faced by the two nuns by visiting Swarkestone bridge and causeway, at DE73 7GW.

The original bridge is thought to have been made of wood, and one legend says its construction was financed by the two Bellamont sisters. Both had become engaged and were to throw a joint celebration; their fiancés, however, had to meet with the local barons on the far side of the river. Following a storm, the Trent became swollen.

The Swarkestone Causeway

Eager to return to their brides-to-be and the betrothal party, the men tried to ford the river on horseback. Both were swept away and drowned.

The Bellamont sisters commissioned the bridge so that no one else would suffer the tragedy they had suffered. Neither sister married and both died in poverty having exhausted their fortune on building the bridge, so naturally their ghosts are reputed to haunt the bridge.

The current stone bridge and causeway was built in the 13th century to cross the river and the surrounding marshes and formed part of the Kings Highway between Derby and Coventry. It is sited at one of the most strategic crossing points, being the main route between Burton and Nottingham for 300 years, and is Grade I Listed and a Scheduled Ancient Monument. At nearly one mile long it is the longest stone bridge, and the longest inland bridge, in England.

As we have seen in Chapter 2, the River Trent served the Vikings as a watery motorway into the heart of Britain. The major barrier between north and south, the river and Swarkestone Bridge have played a significant role throughout history – for example in 1745, Swarkestone Bridge was the southernmost point of Bonny Prince Charlie's advance on London, in his attempt to claim the British throne (and some people allege the bridge is still haunted by Bonnie Prince Charlie's horsemen, with the sound of hooves approaching when nothing is about).

You can see a statue of Bonnie Prince Charlie on horseback at the rear of Derby Cathedral, on Full Street, DE1 3AF. He is looking towards the south, but his horse is already turning back to the north.

04: A Geordie in Exile:

Alkmund

Derby, 8th century

Alkmund was about four years old when his father Alhred was deposed as king of Northumbria, in 774. Alhred fled to Scotland, but his wife Queen Osgifu, and two children Osred and Alkmund, did not go with him. They fled south to Mercia seeking protection. The first major town that they reached was Northworthy, at the place where the Roman road and the River Derwent crossed. Today that town is the City of Derby.

Turmoil in Northumbria continued, and in 788 Osred was chosen to succeed to the throne of Northumbria. Queen Osgifu and Alkmund, who was now 14 years old, returned to the north. After only a year, Osred was deposed and forced into exile on the Isle of Man as a monk. Alkmund was also exiled again.

Early Anglo-Saxon kingdoms were inherently unstable, being based on the king's ability to win battles, conquer territory, and reward his followers (and attract new ones) with land, precious objects and slaves. So civil war amongst the Northumbrians was an unsurprising feature of the next few years, with three more kings in the space of a decade.

Emerging from the turmoil, Eardwulf established his reign as king of Northumberland with a victory in battle at Billington Moor in 798.

Alkmund's role in this civil war is unclear. Mercia did harbour exiles from the north, and may have supported rebels to destabilise its northern neighbour. It seems likely that Alkmund fought in the battle of Billington Moor in an attempt to become king of Northumbria. After defeat, he fled back to Northworthy and into continuing exile. Two years later, in 800, Alkmund was murdered in Northworthy on the orders of Eardwulf. He was buried in the town where he died.

The fighting continued and the king of Mercia, Kenwulf, fought off an invasion by Eardwulf of Northumbria. Unable to make inroads into Northumbrian territory, Kenwulf's revenge came in a different way – he promoted Alkmund as a saint. He established a church of St Alkmund, in which Alkmund was buried in a costly sarcophagus. As this was above ground, it was elaborately decorated on four sides and on the lid.

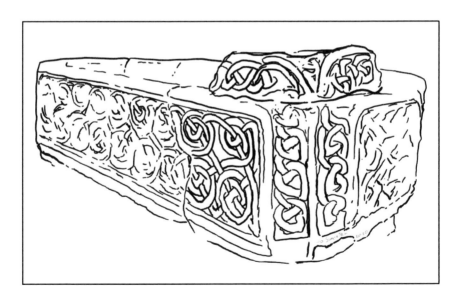

St Alkmund's sarcophagus, displayed in Derby Museum

It seems that by 802, only two years after his murder, Alkmund was already being revered as a saint.

A reputation for charity and care for the poor and orphaned during his exile certainly helped. But turning Alkmund into a saint was a political move. In establishing Alkmund as a saint, with a shrine in Derby, Kenwulf was creating a place where Northumbrians opposed to Eardwulf could gather.

But another piece of political work was also going on – this time on the part of the church. Reacting to political turmoil and violence in both Mercia and Northumbria, in 786 Pope Adrian I sent Legates to both these English kingdoms to establish new laws for their Christian governance. A new canon (a type of church law) accepted in both English kingdoms condemned those responsible for the murder of a king to hell. In practice, the church gave effect to this canon by making royal victims of assassination into saints. The propaganda coup that Alkmund's canonisation gave to Kenwulf of Mercia was part of the church's strategy to discourage such assassinations.

The fighting between and within Mercia and Northumbria ceased soon after Alkmund was declared a saint. And both Kenwulf and Eardwulf reigned for a good length of time and passed on the crown peacefully. Gradually the nature of a king's duties became more wide-ranging than military and judicial roles as life became more settled, so it may be said that the church's policy worked! Alkmund is remembered as the patron saint of Derby – a refugee and victim of political assassination.

A Prayer for Pilgrims

O God, the king of all,

> we give you thanks for Alkmund,
>
> for his acceptance of help and shelter,
>
> for his care for those in need,
>
> and for his witness to peace.

May we follow in the way of Christ

> giving shelter to those far from home,
>
> and building peace between enemies.

We pray for those who are refugees in our world today,

> that they might find a place of safety,
>
> and come to make a home among strangers.

We ask this in the name of Jesus,

> who fled as a refugee to Egypt,
>
> and makes his home amongst us.
>
> Amen.

'Be strong, and let your heart take courage' (Psalm 31:24): a motif from the shaft of St Alkmund's cross, which is displayed in Derby Museum

Where to go

Sites associated with Alkmund in Derby:

St Alkmund's Church on Kedleston Road in Derby, DE22 1GU is the successor to the church of St Alkmund founded by Kenwulf.

The original church was demolished to make way for Derby's inner ring road. Stones from an earlier church on the original site can be seen in the 1970s church on Kedleston Road, and by Jury's Inn hotel on the ring road, at DE1 3DB.

St Alkmund's Well, DE1 3BU on the corner of Well Street and Bath Street, is dedicated to the saint and has been a place of pilgrimage and for the Derbyshire tradition of well dressing. It is said that a vicar of St Werburgh's Church in Derby was cured of consumption by drinking the water of St Alkmund's Well.

St Alkmund's Well

Alkmund's sarcophagus can be seen in the City Museum and Art Gallery on The Strand in Derby, DE1 1BS along with several fragments of the cross shaft from the site.

Derby Cathedral, DE1 3GP has modern red vestments (the colour worn on the feast days of martyrs) which are embroidered with a design from Alkmund's sarcophagus.

Churches elsewhere dedicated to St Alkmund:

There are six churches in England dedicated to St Alkmund. Two are in Derbyshire – the above-mentioned on the Kedleston Road in Derby, and one on Church Drive in Duffield, DE56 4BA.

Also interesting

Symbolism of the hound:

In Celtic and Anglo-Saxon art, artisans took great delight in creating intricate designs of interlaced strapwork and intertwining animals and birds, both natural and mythical.

The type of hunting dog or sight-hound portrayed on Alkmund's cross shaft was known in Britain from Roman times. It is probably an antecedent of the greyhound, deerhound and wolfhound, hunting by sight and speed. Such dogs were strong enough to bring down large beasts, and in later centuries no-one below the status of earl could own one. They are an emblem of royalty, and also of faithfulness and guardianship, and a symbol of a skilled hunter. The emblem was also associated with priests, since priests were watchdogs against the devil.

05: Wolves Calling:

Bertram

Ilam, 8th century

Bertram (also called Beorhthelm or Bertelin) is said to have been a prince of Mercia who left for Ireland in search of a religious calling. It is likely that he was a minor member of the royal family, rather than being an heir apparent who abandoned his duty.

According to an account from the 14th century, he was a friend and pupil of Saint Guthlac. Sometime after Guthlac's death around 715, Bertram established a hermitage on the peninsula named Betheney, which became Stafford. He is said to have converted many to Christianity, and reputedly was able to work miraculous cures through his prayers. The ill-will of jealous detractors led him to relocate to Ilam, in Dovedale, where he eventually died.

However, Bertram's life was not as straightforward as this summary implies, and a number of different stories tell of his adventures and the events that led to him establishing his hermitage.

Ireland was the young Bertram's choice of destination because he was attracted by the stories of St Patrick who had found his calling in Ireland, and Bertram hoped to follow suit. But this was not to be. He found no religious calling, but instead fell in love with a young Irish woman. They eloped and when his wife fell pregnant, Bertram brought her back to Mercia. Travelling through the countryside, she gave birth to their child. In one version of the story, Bertram went to find help and when he returned, he found that both his wife and child had been killed by wolves. A slightly different version says that the new family lived a nomadic life, travelling around the countryside, and that the tragedy happened when Bertram went to hunt for food for the family.

Bertram was distraught, and in his grief he turned to God and vowed to live a life of prayer. He went to the Mercian court, without revealing his royal origins (though his manner and speech would have shown him to be of high rank) and asked for a piece of land to be his hermitage. He was given a piece of land near Stafford.

Later, a new king took the throne of Mercia, and demanded the return of the land on which Bertram had built his hermitage, unless he could beat the king's champion in single combat. As Bertram had turned his back on fighting to become a hermit, he prayed that someone would come forward to fight for the hermitage. He was delighted when a dwarf came forward, as he remembered the Bible story of David and Goliath (1 Samuel 17), in which a small boy defeats a giant. The dwarf duly won, and Bertram kept his land.

Another story tells how the Devil himself tried to tempt Bertram away from his holy life. The Devil showed Bertram some stones and suggested he turn them into bread. Bertram recognised the devil at work, tempting him in the same way that Satan had tempted Jesus in the wilderness (Matthew 4.1-4; Luke 4.1-4). Instead, Bertram prayed that some bread would be turned to stone. As late as the 16th century, these stones were still found in the church at Bartomely, near Crewe in Cheshire. Sadly, they have been lost since then.

Above all, however, Bertram is remembered as a holy man of prayer, who gave wise comfort and advice to those who sought him out. Bertram had gone to Ireland to find his calling but had found love instead. It was in the tragedy of the death of those he loved that he then found his calling. Bertram became a man of prayer and of solitude, and from them became a man of compassion for those around him and a guide for those who needed help. Through prayer and commitment to God, Bertram's tragedy grew into care and healing for those who encountered him.

Perhaps in reaction to the number of people who looked for his help and healing, Bertram left his hermitage near Stafford for a cave in the hills above Ilam. People still found him there, and his reputation as a guide and healer grew. He died in his cave and was buried in the church in Ilam.

St Bertram's tomb is located in a quiet side chapel of the parish church. It became an important place of pilgrimage in medieval times, and people would climb inside to pray for healing. Railings were eventually put around to prevent this. Now people leave their prayer requests on top instead.

51

A Prayer for Pilgrims

God of life and death,

    we give you thanks for Bertram,

    and for his guidance for those in need of help,

    and his compassion for all in pain.

May we follow in the way of Christ,

    finding healing for our hurts,

    and offering care and help to those in need.

We pray for those in grief and despair,

    that they make know your comfort

    and your power to bring life out of death.

We ask this in the name of Jesus,

    who wept for his friend Lazarus,

    and brings new hope to all who fear.

    Amen.

'My eye is wasted from grief; my soul and my body also' (Ps 31:9): a scene from the carvings on the font, showing a creature devouring the mother and child, and St Bertram's Well near the church, below.

Where to go

Bertram just sneaks into a collection of Derbyshire saints, as Ilam is right by the Derbyshire border.

Holy Cross Church in Ilam, DE6 2AZ has Bertram's tomb and shrine in the south chapel. It is still a place of prayer. It has been a place of pilgrimage for centuries (see the 'Also interesting' section).

The carved panels on the magnificent Norman font tell Bertram's story. In addition, the church contains a number of history boards which also tell the story: panel 1 shows the newly married couple, panel 4 Bertram's wife in labour, panels 3 and 6 the wolves devouring the mother and baby, and panel 5 Bertram alone.

St Bertram's Wells:

There are two wells dedicated to St Bertram.

The first is located between the church and St Bertram's Bridge.

St Bertram's Well and Bridge

Go through the gate near the remains of the Saxon crosses in the churchyard and follow the track towards the bridge. It is a rectangular stone pool surrounded by a low stone wall, about half way between the church and the bridge.

The second well is located up on Bunster Hill, and to find it you will need a map and some perseverance (and probably good boots!). The well is one of many in the area that have been a source of fresh water since Saxon times.

Walk through the village and over the river bridge, taking the road leading to Dovedale. The road bends sharply to the right just after the bridge and Home Farm. Climb through the stile on your left. The path branches, well marked to the right to Dovedale, more of a track to the left to the well. Pick your way alongside the drystone walls, steadily climbing along the side of Bunster Hill. The well is easy to spot by the intentional arrangement of stones above it, some of which have remnants of white paint marking them, and the flat-topped stones protecting the watercourse below.

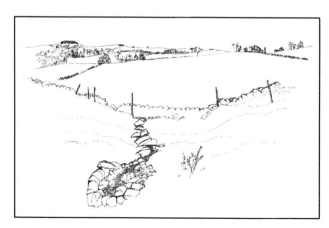

Looking across the valley from St Bertram's Well on Bunster Hill

Also interesting

Bertram retains his association with pilgrimage. The Orthodox churches' annual pilgrimage to Ilam to Bertram's tomb and the wells takes place in August.

The Peak Pilgrimage begins in Ilam.

Details of this is a long-distance walk to Eyam can be found at www.peakpilgrimage.org.uk (see also chapter 8), and a guidebook (with spaces for stamps and stickers from churches along the route) can be ordered from Eyam Parish Church.

06: Carved in Rock:

Cornelius of Depedale and the Cratcliffe Hermits

Dale Abbey and Cratcliffe, 12th-16th centuries

Cornelius of Depedale

Cornelius was a baker in Derby. He was a generous and devout Christian. Every Sunday, he would take anything remaining of his money and food and give it to those in need.

Around the year 1130, Cornelius had a dream. The Virgin Mary appeared to him and said this: 'Acceptable in the eyes of my Son, and of me, are the alms thou hast bestowed. But now, if thou art willing to be made perfect, leave all that thou hast, and go to Depedale where thou shalt serve my Son and me in solitude; and when thou shalt happily have terminated thy course thou shalt inherit the kingdom of love, joy, and eternal bliss which God has prepared for them who love Him'.

Cornelius did not know where Depedale was, so he just walked eastwards away from Derby. At Stanley, he overheard a woman being told to 'take our calves as far as Depedale'. He followed her and settled there. Depedale is now known as Dale Abbey.

What Cornelius found was a marshland, with stony cliffs. To begin with, the hermit dug a place to live in the cliffs in the forest. He probably enlarged an existing cave, finding it offered some immediate shelter and that the relatively soft sandstone was easy to carve. The hermitage he created seems to have a space for prayer, with a niche for a cross and some candles, and a living space.

Shortly after Cornelius had arrived, the landowner, Ralph fitz Geremund, Lord of Ockbrook, rode through the Dale on a hunt. He came across the hermitage and determined to confront the trespasser on his land. Finding the hermit, Ralph was moved by his poverty and impressed by his story. He gave him the cave he had adopted, and granted him a tithe from his mill at Borrowash. This gave Cornelius a small income. The hermit was now a fixture in the Dale. He developed his hermitage, cutting square holes in the rock on the outside of the cave to take poles for a canvas shelter added to enlarge the space. He also dug a well.

Cornelius' hermitage

One story tells of a group of bandits who set up camp near the hermitage. In the night, their leader Uthliglas, had a vision of a golden cross rising from the sky. Finding the hermit, Uthliglas confessed his sins and returned to his fellow robbers. He told them that the cave and the land around was a holy place where they could find God and change their ways. His friends laughed at him and went on their way, but Uthliglas didn't go with them. He had found a new way of life.

Cornelius spent most of his time in prayer and contemplation, and in the work needed to feed himself. As with most of the ancient hermits, the stories of the Depedale hermit speak of his struggles with the devil. Cornelius, alone in prayer, had to contend with his own temptations and propensity to evil. But he also found comfort and provision for his needs: one story tells of Cornelius, weary from the struggles of prayer and in need of water, finding a spring. Near this answer to prayer, he built an oratory and a cottage. These were the beginning of what is now All Saints' Church (which we shall visit again in chapter 13). They were built in about 1150, after Cornelius had been living for twenty years in the cave on the hillside. It was here in his cottage that Cornelius eventually died.

The Cratcliffe Hermits

There is also a hermit's cave below Cratcliffe Rocks, about a mile's walk from Birchover. There is a remarkable crucifix inside, standing about four feet high, carved from the wall of the cave. On the outside of the cave, there are sockets for wooden posts, allowing a shelter to be attached to the cave to enable the hermit to have warmth and a measure of privacy.

The crucifix dates from the 14th century. At that time, hermits were a regular part of the life of the church and local community. They offered hospitality and direction to travellers, and spiritual guidance for visitors and locals alike.

The Hermit's cave and crucifix at Cratcliffe

A Rule of Life for hermits from the 14th century says this: 'Let it suffice thee to have on thine altar an image of the Saviour hanging upon the cross, which represents to thee His passion which thou shalt imitate, inviting thee with outspread arms to himself'.

Hermits were to live with the vision of God's love and invitation to all, and to imitate that in the way they treated others. Virtually nothing is known about the Cratcliffe hermits, but it is clear that there must have been more than one. The crucifix in the cave dates to the 14th century, but the only other piece of evidence about a hermit is in the 16th century, when the accounts of the kitchen of nearby Haddon Hall recorded a payment on 23rd December 1549 to 'Ye Harmytt' for ten rabbits. Another payment of four pence to 'Ye Cratcliffe Hermitte' is recorded for guiding people to Haddon Hall. Clearly, the hermit of the time had found ways to support his isolated life by trapping rabbits and guiding travellers. But between the 14th and mid 16th centuries, more than one person will have lived as a hermit in Cratcliffe.

The life of a hermit was and is one of withdrawal from the world and from other people. In the isolation of a hermitage the hermit has solitude in which to spend time in the presence of God. The crucifix that the Cratcliffe hermits had to gaze upon, as well as being a stunning and beautiful piece of art, would have been a daily reminder of the lengths to which God went to reach out to us in love. The death of Jesus is the greatest sign of God's love for the world. The daily contemplation of this sign in the silence of the hermitage did not increase the isolation of the hermits. Rather it led the hermits to imitate that love, and to give themselves for the sake of others. Guidance and counsel, prayer and practical support for others would have been regular parts of the hermits' lives. But always behind this activity stands the silence and solitude in which they daily renewed their lives in the shape of the crucifix carved on the wall.

A Prayer for Pilgrims

God of solitude and love,

  we give you thanks for Cornelius and for the Cratcliffe hermits,

  for their silence and prayer

  and for their imitation of your love in Jesus.

May we follow in the way of Christ,

  seeking your presence in solitude and simplicity of life,

  and sharing your love with those we meet.

We pray for those who seek solitude today,

  that they may encounter you in silence,

  and find new strength for serving others.

We ask this in the name of Jesus

  who fasted in the wilderness

  and withdrew from the crowds to pray.

  Amen.

The hermit's forage pot: a medieval cooking pot with herbs illustrated in a Tudor herbal: foxglove, bramble, ramsons, dandelion, tansy, clover and mint.

Where to go

Cornelius

Dale Abbey is about six miles northeast of Derby.

All Saints' Church, DE7 4PN stands on the edge of the village. The key to the church is held in one of the houses you will pass, and a noticeboard on the edge of the churchyard gives details of this. The church is a remarkable space. From the 17th century, it developed a tradition of puritan and protestant preachers that continues today. (See Chapter 13 for more details.)

Go past the church of All Saints and into the Hermit's Wood. This is an area of Special Scientific Interest, remarkable for its different species of lime trees. It is also a remnant of Sherwood Forest that covered most of Derbyshire at one time.

Follow the path up into the Wood, and you will come to the hermitage, signposted 'Hermit's Cave'. (The other end of the footpath is on Potato Pit Lane, opposite the T-junction with Dale Rd.) The altar niche and a simple cross are clearly visible carved into the walls of the cave.

The Hermit's Well is close to the hermitage. This is a spring-fed well, and although it is on private land, in winter it can be seen clearly from the path. Medieval traditions suggest that drinking from the well three times between 12 noon and 3pm on Good Friday (the last three hours of Jesus' earthly life) was believed to cure illness and disease.

The Cratcliffe Hermits

The Cratcliffe hermitage stands at the foot of Cratcliffe Rocks on the edge of Harthill Moor and near Nine Stones Circle and Robin Hood's Stride. It's an extensive area of rocks and woodland with good views from the tops. There are two directions of approach.

Cratcliffe Parking area, DE4 2LZ is on the B5056 nearby, and there is also a bus stop for Dudwood Farm. Follow the lane to Dudwood Farm. Where it forks left to become the Limestone Way, continue right for the Caves. It's a steepish walk down to the caves.

Or approach from the other end of the Limestone Way. On the road from Elton to Alport (Cliff Lane), stop near Harthill Moor Farm, DE45 1LL. A path from there runs down to the foot of Robin Hood's Stride, and in the opposite direction the path leads up to the Cratcliffe Crags and the Caves. Find out more about the Limestone Way in the 'Also interesting' section.

The Hermit's Cave has been much used as a shelter and is now fenced off with iron railings to prevent further damage to the carving. Look for the sockets on the outside of the cave where wooden poles would have been attached at some point in the life of the hermitage.

Also interesting

Dale Abbey:

After Cornelius had died, a woman known as the Gomme, or godmother, of the Dale developed his cottage and oratory. Now recognised as a holy place, Dale attracted an Abbey, founded in 1204. A formal monastic community, called white canons because of the colour of their robes, served as parish priests for the surrounding villages of Kirk Hallam, Stanton-by-Dale, Ilkeston and Heanor. At this point Depedale became known as Dale Abbey. The Abbey was closed as part of Henry VIII's dissolution of the monasteries in 1539. The abbey buildings were sold, and stone from them was removed for other buildings. Today a solitary arch remains.

Dale Abbey arch

A local Gretna Green:

Dale Abbey has a particular history connected with weddings. The stories of Robin Hood tell of Dale as the place where Allan-a-Dale was married. After the closure of the Abbey, the church in Dale Abbey was never given into the control of the diocesan bishop (at that time in Lichfield). Consequently, marriages could be performed with minimal notice, and Dale Abbey became the Gretna Green of the midlands.

The Limestone Way:

Cratcliffe also has a Robin Hood connection: it's located near Robin Hood's Stride, a gritstone outcrop from the top of which you can see one of several prehistoric stone circles in the area.

The Limestone Way was created by local people to show off their landscape. It runs for 46 miles from Castleton down to Tissington and then on into a flatter stretch in Staffordshire.

The section south from Youlgreave, which is just south of Bakewell, can be done in a day, and passes near the Cratcliffe hermits' cave. Part of this section follows the traces of a prehistoric road, the Portway. This ancient track contours intuitively across the landscape showing where thousands of years of humans, horses and cattle have passed, gradually bedding their path deep into the ground.

A fashion for hermitages:

In the 18th century, hermitages were very fashionable amongst the gentry of Derbyshire. At Dale Abbey, the hermitage was used by the Stanhope family to entertain guests, and at Cratcliffe, the local vicar saw fit to install viewing terraces and stone armchairs.

At the same time, the Anchor Church near Ingleby (see Chapter 3), became a venue for parties for the landlord of Foremark Hall.

Kedleston Hall indulged the fashion with a faux hermitage in its grounds, which has been recently restored.

The Chatsworth estate eschewed the fashion for a hermitage. But in 1789 Duchess Georgiana, wife of the 5th Duke of Devonshire, added a Grotto which was lined with some of her collection of minerals and fossils. At about the furthest point of the gardens away from the house, it is still a place of relative quiet, even on the busiest bank holiday.

07: Deaths in the Family: The Reformation Martyrs: Joan Waste, Ralph Sherwin, Nicholas Garlick, Robert Ludlum, Richard Simpson, Christopher Buxton, Edward James and William Hartley

Derby, Rodsley, Longford, Tideswell and Padley, 16th century

In the late autumn of 1517, Martin Luther published his 95 Theses, which were arguments against some of the practices of the Roman Catholic Church. This has been taken as the opening salvo of the Reformation – a movement within Christianity that brought new life and vitality to the faith, but at the cost of division and at times open warfare.

Evangelicals or Protestants proclaimed the free grace and forgiveness of God, a return to the Bible in the language of the people, and an end to many long-established practices such as prayers for the dead, penance for sins, the Latin Mass and the authority of the Pope.

Whereas in Europe, Protestantism came from the rebellion of people to religious authority, in England the Reformation was largely dictated by the crown. In the 1530s, Henry VIII, previously a staunch supporter of the Catholic Church against the Protestant reforms, enacted a serious of measures which broke completely with the authority of Rome, but allowed little else to change.

However, the *status quo* did not last long. Henry VIII's heir Edward VI introduced thoroughgoing Protestantism to England. His half-sister

Mary Tudor, who succeeded him, restored Catholicism. Then Elizabeth I settled England as a Protestant country.

Each side regarded the other with suspicion, and at every stage there was violence. Protestants were burnt as heretics by Catholics. Because of the involvement of the crown in the religious status of the country, Catholics were usually executed as traitors. This was made more likely when Pope Pius V issued a letter in 1570 excommunicating Queen Elizabeth and releasing her subjects from allegiance to her. Anti-Catholic paranoia on the part of the government led to continued bursts of persecution continuing well into the 17th century. All of this religious doctrine and high politics was felt across the country, including in Derbyshire.

These eight Derbyshire saints, one Protestant and seven Catholic, died for the Christian faith as they understood it. This civil war within Christianity had a very human cost. That a religion based on love and peace contained such murderous possibility should give us pause to reflect and to mourn.

Joan Waste

Joan was a blind girl born in 1534, the daughter of William Waste a barber and rope maker. Joan and her twin brother Roger helped make rope to support the family finances. Living in the parish of St Peter's Derby, Joan enjoyed hearing the Bible read from an English translation. Such was her love of the Bible that she saved her money and bought a copy of her own. She would ask the clerk of the church to read to her, and when he was not available would even pay others to read to her.

A change in government brought Joan into conflict with the newly restored Catholic Church. She was arrested in June 1556. At her trial before the Bishop of Lichfield in All Saints' Church in Derby, she was accused of holding false views about the Holy Communion. To the sophisticated theology that was spoken to her, Joan replied that she believed what she read in the Bible and what had been taught by (Protestant) preachers that she had heard.

She told the Bishop that she would change her view if he would answer for her at the Day of Judgement. The Bishop was about to agree to this, when his Chancellor told him that he could not. Turning to Joan, the Chancellor asked her if she would answer for herself. Joan said that if the Bishop would not take responsibility for what he was asking her to believe then she was willing to die for her faith.

The trial was concluded, and Joan was condemned to death. On 1st August 1556, Joan was brought back from the prison to All Saints' Church where the Chancellor preached a sermon to her, telling her that she would burn in hell for eternity. He also forbade anyone to pray for her.

He then sent her on a cart to the execution site, while he is said to have returned to his inn to sleep. Joan held the hand of her twin brother while she said her final prayers, asked those present to pray for her (despite the Chancellor's sermon), and was then burned at Windmill Hill Pit.

Ralph Sherwin

Ralph Sherwin was born at Rodsley in Derbyshire in 1550 and was christened in Longford Church. His parents, John and Constance, who were convicted for Catholic beliefs after Ralph's death, were at this stage conforming to the Protestant rules of the Elizabethan church.

Ralph's parents sent him to Eton College. From there, in 1568, he went to Exeter College in Oxford where he proved to be an excellent scholar. His skills in public debating caught the attention of the Earl of Leicester (then a favourite of Queen Elizabeth). In 1570, Exeter College was visited by a Royal Commission and both the Rector and Dean were imprisoned for their Catholic beliefs.

Sherwin graduated as a Master of Arts in 1574. One year later, pretending to be going to study medicine, Ralph travelled to Douai in France to train for the Catholic priesthood. He was ordained on 23rd March 1577, and almost immediately set out for Rome as the first student of the new English College in Rome.

In Rome, Ralph proved a radical. He was instrumental in shaping the English College to be a training ground for Catholic missionaries to England. In April 1580, he took the missionary oath, declaring himself ready 'today rather than tomorrow' to return to England for the saving of souls.

On 1st August 1580, Ralph sailed for England and secretly travelled about preaching and celebrating mass. He managed to be engaged in this mission clandestinely for about three months, until on 4th November, he was caught preaching at the house of a friend from university, Nicholas Roscarrock.

Taken to Marshalsea gaol, Ralph continued to preach and convert people to the Catholic faith. At a hearing of the case of treason against him, he called out, 'The plain reason for our standing here is religion not treason'.

A month later he was taken to the Tower of London, where he was tortured by the authorities seeking evidence against Roscarrock and Mary Queen of Scots. Having established that he would not give them any information, the authorities tried to get him to conform. His brother was brought in to persuade him, and Ralph told him about a vision of standing at the foot of the cross looking up into Jesus' eyes. It is even suggested that Queen Elizabeth personally offered Ralph a bishopric if he would conform to the Protestant church.

After a year in prison, he was tried for treason at Westminster Hall and then executed at Tyburn in London on 1st December 1581. Whilst waiting for his sentence to be carried out, Ralph's letters show an impatience for martyrdom to come. As he stood at the foot of the scaffold, Ralph protested his innocence and forgave those whose actions had led to his death. He prayed for the Queen (a final controversy, because he prayed for her to become a Catholic) and was then hanged, drawn and quartered. His final words were *'Jesu, Jesu, Jesu, esto mihi Jesus!'* (best understood as 'Jesus, Jesus, Jesus, be to me a saviour').

The Padley Martyrs: Nicholas Garlick, Robert Ludlum and Richard Simpson

Nicholas Garlick was born at Dinting, near Glossop in 1555. He apparently moved to Tideswell because he had fallen in love with a girl he saw when he was out walking. It did not to amount to anything, partly because the girl actually lived in Eyam.

Nicholas started studies at Gloucester Hall (now Worcester College) in Oxford, but only stayed six months as he was appointed schoolmaster at Tideswell School in 1575: his family had sold land to the school when it was founded.

In 1579, whilst walking in Monksdale, Nicholas vowed to devote his life to the Catholic faith. He set out for Rheims and trained for ministry there. He was ordained in 1582 and sent back to England in 1583. After a spy (also from Tideswell) reported him, Nicholas was deported to the continent in 1585. He returned to Rheims but after only two days set out once more for England. This second mission to England lasted two years, and he is known to have been diligent about ministry in London, Hampshire, Dorset and Derbyshire. On 12th July 1588, he was arrested at Padley Manor House, the home of John Fitzherbert.

Another priest was also arrested that night, Robert Ludlum. Robert was born in Radbourne in Derbyshire and attended St John's College in Oxford. He left without taking a degree, possibly because he would have had to take the Oath of Supremacy to do so, acknowledging the English monarch as the official head of the Church of England, supplanting the power of the Catholic Pope in Rome.

Robert travelled to Rheims in 1580 and was ordained priest in 1581. The following year he returned to England. The lack of knowledge of his ministry in England is a sign of its success in the secrecy needed for a Catholic priest.

However, at Padley Manor House Robert's luck ran out. Arrested with Nicholas Garlick, the two were taken to Derby. One story has it that on their way there, passing through Eyam, they were mocked and insulted by the crowd so that one of them uttered a curse that was taken as a prediction of the plague that afflicted Eyam in the following century (see Chapter 8).

In Derby, the pair were held in a cell with a third priest, Richard Simpson. He was a Yorkshireman, and had been a priest in the Church of England before converting to Catholicism. After a time in prison in York, he had gone to Douai to train for the Catholic priesthood and been ordained in Brussels in 1577. Returning to England, he ministered in Lancashire and Derbyshire. Like Nicholas Garlick, he was deported in 1585 but returned to England.

In January 1588 he was betrayed by a man in the Peak District pretending to be a Catholic, and taken to Derby where he was sentenced to death. The sentence was not carried out immediately, and some accounts suggest that Richard was on the verge of conforming when Nicholas and Robert were placed in his cell. The two more recently arrested men strengthened Richard in his faith and brought him back to the Catholic fold. On the night before the three died, they were held with a woman convicted for murder. Speaking to the three priests, she was reconciled to God and confessed her faith before she was executed.

Nicholas Garlick, Robert Ludlum and Richard Simpson were executed on 24th July 1588, at St Mary's Bridge in Derby. Arriving at the execution site, the executioners were not ready. Nicholas used the time to preach a sermon to the crowd, and then threw into the crowd some tracts which he had written in prison to explain the faith. He was the first to be executed, kissing the ladder before climbing up the scaffold. Richard died next, and was found to be wearing a hair shirt as a sign of penance. Finally Robert, who was smiling with joy throughout, was killed. Nicholas Garlick's head was later taken from its pole and buried surreptitiously in Tideswell churchyard.

The Padley martyrs were the first executions of Catholic priests after a pause of about ten months. The news of Philip II of Spain's plans for an invasion of England had led the government to suspend executions, perhaps to remove one of his complaints. Once the Armada had failed, however, the executions began again with a vengeance.

Nicholas Garlick kissing the ladder to the scaffold, at the execution of the three Padley Martyrs near the Bridge Chapel in 1588, as portrayed in a window in St Mary's Catholic Church in Derby.

Christopher Buxton, Edward James and William Hartley

As well as the three Padley martyrs, three other Catholic priests from Derbyshire were executed.

Christopher Buxton, born 1562 in Tideswell, was a student of Nicholas Garlick there. In 1582 he travelled with two school friends to Rheims to study for ordination. From there he went to the English College in Rome, where he was ordained in 1586. In September of the following year, he landed in Kent. He was arrested in Sittingbourne in November 1587 and sent to Newgate and then to Marshalsea prison. Whilst in the Marshalsea, he wrote a Rituale, a liturgical text, which he sent to a priest friend. This is preserved at Olney in Buckinghamshire as a relic.

Christopher was questioned and admitted being a priest. He was executed with two companions on 1st October 1588 at Oaten Hill in Canterbury. He was offered the chance to save his life by conforming, but replied, 'I will not purchase corruptible life at so dear a rate; and indeed, if I had a hundred lives, I would willingly lay down all in defence of my Faith'.

Edward James was born at Barton, Breaston, near Long Eaton. He was educated at Derby School and St John's College, Oxford. Like Christopher Buxton, he trained for ministry in Rheims and at the English College in Rome. He was ordained priest in October 1583. After returning to England, he and three other priests were captured on board a ship at Littlehampton in Sussex in 1586 and held for two years without trial in London.

After the failure of the Armada, the four were tried. One conformed and was spared, James and another two were condemned to death. On 1st October 1588, they were taken for execution at Broyle Heath, near Chichester. Another of the priests recanted in the face of the scaffold and was spared. James and the other priest absolved each other and were then executed.

The final Derbyshire martyr of the Reformation is William Hartley. Born at Wyn (or Wilne) to a yeoman (landowning) family in 1557, Hartley went to St John's College in Oxford where he became a chaplain and fellow. He was ejected in 1579 on suspicion of being a Catholic. The suspicions were presumably true, because he went immediately to Rheims and was ordained as a Catholic priest in Châlons.

He returned to England in 1580 and was part of a network printing and distributing books by other Catholic priests. He was arrested in 1581 and sent to the Marshalsea prison. Even here Hartley was caught saying Mass in his cell.

In 1585, he was exiled and returned to Rheims, before making a pilgrimage to Rome. Returning to active mission within England in 1586, he worked for nearly two years before being arrested in September 1588 in Holborn in London. He was executed at Tyburn on 5th October 1588.

The martyrdoms of these eight people are horrific and gruesome. Burning people to death, or hanging, drawing and quartering them, are intentionally appalling ways to be killed. That this was done by Christian to Christian, whatever differences in understanding of the faith, adds a new level of horror.

Joan Waste, killed for her simple reading of the Bible, and the seven Catholic priests murdered for praying and preaching, all witness to the practice of faith in Jesus Christ. It is that faith that is inspiring, even in the face of death.

In 1970 Pope Paul VI declared forty Catholic martyrs of the Reformation, including Ralph Sherwin, to be saints. He spoke of them 'advancing an ecumenism worthy of the name'. Christians of all traditions must face the hard truths of our divisions and the violence that has been, and continues to be, inflicted in the name of Christ.

A Prayer for Pilgrims

God of truth and of compassion,

We give you thanks for Joan Waste, Ralph Sherwin, Nicholas Garlick,

Robert Ludlum, Richard Simpson, Christopher Buxton, Edward

James and William Hartley, and for all who died as martyrs in the

Reformation.

We thank you for their faith in Jesus Christ,

and for the courage of their witness to him.

May we follow in the way of Christ,

being courageous in our witness to truth,

and learning to live alongside those who disagree with us.

We pray for those who are persecuted for their faith and belief today,

that they may have courage to stand for the truth,

and protection from those who would harm them.

We ask this in the name of Jesus,

who prayed for forgiveness for those who killed him.

Amen.

Burning with zeal for the Lord: an image drawn from the commemorative plaque to Joan Waste at the site of her execution.

Where to go

Joan Waste

There is still a court (albeit a 17th century one) to the left side of the choir in Derby Cathedral, DE1 3GP where Joan Waste was tried and condemned – though the only part of the building surviving from that time is the imposing tower.

The family attended St Peter's Church (DE1 1NN).

Recalling the healing between traditions that has occurred since the violence of the Reformation, there is another plaque commemorating Joan in the garden of St Joseph's Catholic Church, DE1 1TJ, which stands on the site of her execution at Windmill Pit on the Burton Road. Much further afield, there is a plaque remembering Joan in St Michael's Church in Birchover, DE4 2BG.

Ralph Sherwin

In Rodsley, DE6 3AN a plaque commemorates Ralph Sherwin's birthplace. The font where he was christened is still in use in Longford Church, DE6 3DS. The Ralph Sherwin Society (www.ralphsherwin.com) organise a pilgrimage to Rodsley one Sunday in June each year. It is normally led by the Catholic Bishop of Nottingham.

There was a church dedicated to St Ralph Sherwin in Swarkestone Road, Chellaston, but it was demolished and a supermarket now occupies the site. The church housed a painting of Ralph, based on a contemporary description used by the authorities to hunt him. The whereabouts of the painting is currently unknown, but there are plans to build another church.

Ralph also appears in windows in St Mary's Catholic Church in Derby, DE1 3AX. St Joseph's Catholic Church, also in Derby, DE1 1TJ has a side chapel with a beautiful window of him; the chapel also contains some of his relics.

The Padley Martyrs

St Mary's Catholic Church, DE1 3AX has windows of the Padley Martyrs as well as Ralph Sherwin.

A commemoration of the Padley martyrs is also found on the side of the Chapel of St Mary on the Bridge, DE1 3DD beside the site of their execution in Derby.

The Chapel of St Mary on the Bridge
with remains of the original bridge visible beneath

83

The Padley martyrs are remembered in the church at Tideswell, SK17 8NU, the home of Nicholas Garlick and his pupil Christopher Buxton. Garlick's head is buried in the churchyard.

At Padley, near Grindleford, the ruins of Padley Manor and its chapel can be found at S32 2JA. Access to the site can be arranged through the Catholic Diocese of Hallam Pastoral Centre (0114 256 6401) and there is an annual pilgrimage to the site in July.

As a group:

St Mary's Catholic Church in Derby, DE1 3AX has windows depicting Ralph Sherwin, Christopher Buxton and the Padley Martyrs together, though not including Edward James or William Hartley.

Ecumenical commemoration:

On the 24th July each year, or very near to that date, an ecumenical service commemorating the Padley Martyrs and Joan Waste is held in the Bridge Chapel, Derby DE1 3AX.

08: Trembling before the Lord:

John Gratton, Margaret Lyman and Derbyshire's Quakers

Bonsall, Matlock, Monyash, Derby, Crich, Darby Pennsylvania, 17th-18th centuries

John Gratton

John Gratton (1641-1711/2) was born at Bonsall near Cromford. His father appears to have been a prosperous yeoman or farmer. As a boy John kept his father's sheep and took great delight 'in playing cards, and shooting at bulls and ringing of bells' but also felt within himself a spiritual questioning.

His Journal, published in 1719, tells of his desperate and agonising pursuit for true Christianity, picking his way with anger and dismay amongst the many Protestant sects and denominations of the day. After nearly a decade of civil war, England was ruled as a Commonwealth in the 1650s. Oliver Cromwell ruled a republican government, exercising monarchical powers as Lord Protector. The Church of England with its bishops and priests had been swept away and a Presbyterian style of parish governance put in place. Following decades of religious upheaval, many people were questioning the established principles and teachings of former scholars and the church. Free-thinkers were questioning the ethics of religion and authority, and small groups of these dissenters met for worship and discussion, often in their own homes.

John explored all the options open to him. He listened to various preachers and read pious books without obtaining religious peace. He joined the Presbyterians, but was 'unable to sing psalms truthfully'.

After the Restoration of the monarchy in 1660 and the Act of Uniformity which re-established the Church of England, he frequented the church. He disliked the set forms of prayer in the newly revised Book of Common Prayer, finding the liturgy barren and lifeless. For a while he attended various dissenting conventicles and engaged in debate with their preachers. Next, he joined an anabaptist congregation until it was broken up under the provisions of the Conventicle Act. This Act imposed a fine on any person who attended any religious assembly other than the Church of England, and on any preacher or person who allowed their house to be used as a meeting place for such an assembly.

One of the matters he most struggled with was the doctrine of predestination, prevalent throughout the Protestant churches. This stated that God had fore-ordained a small number of individuals to be saved and had therefore condemned the rest of humanity to eternal damnation. John, on the contrary, was convinced that those who were 'in Christ' were elected, but those who were 'out of Christ were out of the way to God' and he concluded: 'For Christ is the elect and chosen of God, the heir of all things, and all that are in him are co-heirs with him'. Furthermore, he roundly condemned what he called 'hireling clergy' saying, 'But if Christ be not in them, then they are reprobates, without God in the world, dead in sins and trespass, and so all they do are dead works, dead prayers, dead preaching, dead worship and performances'. He was a very angry young man.

In about 1670 John married, and shortly afterwards the couple went to live at Monyash in Derbyshire. John joined the Quaker society at Matlock, finding at last a group that emphasised the importance of a personal and direct religious experience of Christ. They valued both direct religious experience and the reading and studying of the Bible. They focused their private life on developing behaviour and speech reflecting emotional purity and the light of God though piety, faith, and love. At last he experienced his 'road to Damascus' moment and he wrote in his journal, 'I have found the Pearl of great price, the one thing needful for my soul to know, and this is Christ within, the hope of glory, the true way to the Father, who promised to be with his disciples to the end of the world... Oh that the children of men would open their hearts... Then they would come to witness the Comforter, the Spirit of Truth, to lead them into all truth; for it is he who works all our works in us and for us...'.

John became a recognised preacher, making many ministerial journeys over the next twenty-five years. He had a number of narrow escapes from arrest under the Conventicle Act, and related that, on the understanding that the meetings were silent, the Friends were protected by constables. He was fined several times for preaching, but, owing to the respect in which he was held, these fines were rarely enforced. However, about 1680, he was served with a writ of excommunication, and was subsequently lodged in Derby Gaol, though being leniently treated. He lay in prison, he says, 'quietly till King James set me at liberty' in 1686.

Eventually ill-health compelled him to give up regular journeys. Early in 1707 he disposed of his estate at Monyash, and went to reside with his son, Joseph Gratton, at or near Farnsfield in Nottinghamshire, where, in December of that year, his wife died at the age of sixty-eight.

After one more journey, he finally settled with his daughter Phœbe Bateman, at Farnsfield. After much suffering, he died on 9th March 1711 or 1712. He was buried by the side of his wife in the Quaker burial-ground at Farnsfield.

Gratton was a man of high character: pious, unassuming and charitable. His Journal has frequently been reprinted; it gives valuable descriptions of village life in a pleasing style. He shows us the value of persistence in the search for personal knowledge of Jesus Christ, and once having found that 'pearl of great price' to follow the leadings of the Holy Spirit to share that faith and to witness to it by a sincere and faithful life, even if it brings suffering. His gentleness led his gaolers to be respectful towards him, but that had not been the case in earlier decades, when prayer meetings were broken up and people fined for not attending church or paying tithes to the priest. Nevertheless, their patience and forbearance were notable.

Margaret Lyman

In the years leading up to John's imprisonment in Derby Gaol, the Quakers of Crich, Fritchley and Whatstandwell had suffered particularly from the enthusiastic suppression of their meetings by the local soldiers and clergy. They logged their grievances from 1650, when George Fox was imprisoned in Derby Gaol (see 'Also interesting' at the end of this chapter) to 1690, a year after the Act of Toleration was passed in the first year of the reign of William and Mary.

They held a firm belief in the priesthood of all believers, citing the First Epistle of Peter: 'you are .... a royal priesthood, a holy nation, God's own people, in order that you may proclaim the mighty acts of him who called you out of darkness into his marvellous light' (1 Peter 2.9). Their refusal to pay tithes to support the local clerics, attend public church services, bear arms or swear oaths, combined with their constant calmly reasoned challenges to authority, led to the prevailing Protestant view that they were a blasphemous challenge to social and political order. This led to judicial persecution in England and Wales.

Besides repeated imprisonments, the punishments were fines and confiscation of goods, and public humiliations such as the stocks or pillory, often accompanied by whippings, stonings and both physical and verbal abuse. These were sometimes led by the local priest, and were administered to women as well as men.

Eyam stocks

On 23rd June 1661, a barn in Crich was used to imprison a party of forty-one Quakers from the Eyam area overnight, *en route* to Derby Gaol. No transport was provided, they had to walk accompanied by four constables. On this, the second night in custody, they were put into Squire Claye's barn without food or water.

By chance, 10-year-old Samuel Lynam was bringing cows down to a better pasture when he spotted the group in the marketplace and was curious because they did not look like felons. Taking a closer look, he recognised several neighbours and realised they must have been in a meeting the day before, which had been broken up (meetings of more than five were forbidden). Samuel ran back to his aunt's farm in Fritchley with the news. His aunt was Margaret Lyman, an eloquent Quaker preacher. Her husband, his uncle John, was currently in Derby goal for failing to pay tithes to the priest of South Wingfield, so Samuel knew the implications of what he had seen.

Margaret and two of the farm workers gathered cheese and whatever bread, oatcakes and milk they could carry, and set out to relieve the necessities of their suffering brothers and sisters, and bring some comfort and cheer. On the way they left messages to be sent to others on the probable route to Derby so that the group could be similarly sustained through the rest of their march. Next morning, they sent them off with a good breakfast augmented by contributions from Quakers in neighbouring villages.

There were fears and forebodings. A contemporary document warns that, 'Episcopacy was again established, and the iron hand of the Bishops was increasingly being felt' but above all these discouragements was the assurance that the protecting arms of the Lord were around them, and that he would not fail to sustain in every time of need.

Margaret walked with the group as far as Fritchley and sent a message of loving encouragement to her imprisoned husband. In Derby two of the group were singled out for particularly vicious treatment by the gaoler, being 'inhumanly used by the cruel keeper, who put them into a close Hole where they could not stand upright, nor had they Liberty to come out to ease their Bodies, but were constrained to do it in the Place. Their Books and Letters were taken away and never restored. And when in that strait Confinement they were praying to the Lord, the Keeper in a Rage would strike them on the face, and attempt to stop their Mouths; nor were their Friends permitted either to visit or relieve them'.

The group was held for a month and then released along with John. Two years later, Margaret's husband was again prosecuted by the vicar of South Wingfield. But faithfully and steadily the couple were enabled to bear their testimony for nearly thirty years, until in 1677, weary of the continued persecution, they sailed from Hull for Pennsylvania on the fly boat 'Martha'. And that is why there is a town called Darby in the USA, a few miles from Philadelphia, founded by Derbyshire Quaker families in 1682.

A Prayer for Pilgrims

God of patience and forbearance,

    we give you thanks for John Gratton, Margaret Lyman and the

    Quakers of Derbyshire,

    for their courage in preaching and speaking the truth,

    and for their provision for those in need.

May we follow in the way of Christ,

    patiently seeking the light of revelation in our hearts

    and serving you in every person.

We pray for all who are imprisoned today,

    that they might be treated with justice,

    and find hope and light in the darkest of places.

We ask this in the name of Jesus,

    who is the Light of the World, that has never been overcome.

    Amen.

The barn at Crich, and a basket of local provender

Where to go

John Gratton

Matlock Friends Meeting House: Jackson Road / Jackson Tor Road, DE4 3JQ. Founded in 1720 and now in residential use.

Monyash: The Grade 2 listed Friends Meeting House and burial ground are in Chapel Street, DE45 1JJ. The meeting house was erected shortly after John Gratton's death, in 1717.

Derby Gaol: Edward II granted Derby town the right to have a gaol in 1327. The Cornmarket Gaol where the individuals mentioned in this chapter were held no longer exists. However, Friargate Gaol, DE1 1DF has a museum, and the impressive frontage of the Vernon Street Goal with its two Martello towers is worth seeing - at the junction of Vernon Street and South Street, DE1 1UJ.

Margaret Lyman

Crich: Squire Claye's Barn is visible behind St Mary's Church, Cromford Road, DE4 5DJ.

Fritchley: The Lyman's farm is at Tithe Farm, Lyman Road, DE56 2HQ, to the west of Fritchley, on a lane which leads to Fritchley Friends Meeting House, DE56 2FR.

Eyam: The stocks still stand on the village green at S32 5QW. Miscreants would be held in the stocks by their legs or arms and heads and pelted with stones and clods of earth or more smelly missiles such as offal and dung.

Also interesting

Monyash and Well Dressing:

The town became important in Roman times because it was at the intersection of a number of trade routes, and evidence of medieval farming can be seen in its layout and also the identifiable pattern of crofts and strip fields running from the main streets.

The name Monyash comes from the Old English words 'Mane' and 'Eas', meaning many waters. In the past the village had no less than five ponds and twenty wells. Unsurprisingly therefore, Monyash is one of the villages that celebrates Derbyshire's distinctive tradition of well dressing. Dressing and blessing wells originally started as a thanksgiving for the gift of water, especially in times of drought. The dressings are intricate pictures in which local natural materials such as flower petals, mosses, leaves, twigs and small stones, are pressed into a clay base within a wooden frame. Three wells are decorated in Monyash during the May Day holiday.

George Fox in Derby Gaol and the origin of the term 'Quaker':

Thirty years prior to John Gratton's stay in Derby Gaol, George Fox, the founder of the Quakers, was imprisoned under the Blasphemy Act of 1650, for a year. He had attended a lecture in Derby among 'an abundance of the officers of the army, and priests and preachers'. When the preacher had finished Fox asked leave to speak and talked of 'the day of the Lord, and the light within them, and the spirit to teach and lead them to God' after which he was taken before the magistrates 'charged with the avowed uttering and broaching of divers blasphemous opinions, contrary to a late Act of Parliament'. It was at the arraignment that the magistrate, Mr Justice Bennet, ridiculed him and 'was the first that called us Quakers, because I bade them tremble at the word of the Lord'.

During his imprisonment he was kept in a dungeon 'among thirty felons in a lousy, stinking low place in the ground without any bed' though with occasional walks in the garden, and although he was offered the chance of release if he agreed to serve in Cromwell's army, he refused. While in prison he wrote and reflected.

There is a blue plaque on the side of the Friends Meeting House in Derby at 56 St Helen's St, DE1 3HY, recording Fox's encounter with the magistrate in 1650.

09: The Village of the Saved:

Eyam and the Plague

Eyam, 1665-1666

In late August 1665, a box of clothes from London arrived in the village of Eyam. The clothes were last season's, discarded by the fashionable people of London. But in Derbyshire, they could yet inspire. They had been ordered by a tailor, one Alexander Hadfield, who was hoping to use the clothes as patterns for new custom in Derbyshire. Hadfield, however, did not open the box. His assistant George Viccars unpacked the clothes and hung them to dry. Soon he became unwell, and on 6th September, he died. Plague had arrived in Eyam.

Plague is a virulent disease, spread by the fleas on rats. It reached Europe in the 14th century and was a deadly and much feared disease. This outbreak was raging in London during 1665-6, eventually killing a hundred thousand people, and now it had reached Eyam.

By the end of September 1665, a further five people had died, and in October a further twenty-three deaths were recorded. Winter was known to bring relief, which to a certain extent it did, but the death toll continued to mount.

By the end of April 1666, there had been 73 deaths. But then there was hope. In May there were only four deaths, two of which were not from plague. News from London was that the plague there was over (even the king had thought it safe to return in February). But the plague was not done in Eyam.

In the midst of this distress, visiting the sick, burying the dead and comforting those who mourn, was William Mompesson, the Rector of Eyam. Mompesson, however, was not a popular Rector. He had only arrived in Eyam in 1664, so was new and still trying to build up trust with the villagers. This was made more difficult by the presence of Thomas Stanley. Stanley had been the Rector of Eyam between 1644 and 1660. But Stanley was a puritan, and did not accept (that is, 'dissented from') the restoration of the Church of England at the end of the Commonwealth, so had been ejected from the parish.

The Parish had been united in petitioning the patron for him to remain in 1660. The petition was unsuccessful, and the Act of Uniformity of 1662, which introduced the revised Book of Common Prayer, was the end of Stanley's role in Eyam. Or so it seemed. It is clear that Stanley ignored the law that forbade dissenting clergy from coming within five miles of their former parishes. And in the midst of the plague, Mompesson reached out to Stanley for help.

Mompesson and Stanley, from two very different religious traditions, came together in the service of the village. Neither could have brought the village together alone. Mompesson, the youthful stranger who was now the Rector, would not have won enough of the trust of the village. Stanley, the older dissenter and former Rector, no longer had the authority. However, together they were able to make plans, to gather the village, and to ensure that everyone held to the decisions taken.

On 24th June 1666, Mompesson and Stanley led the village in making three resolutions.

The first was that there would be no more organised funerals. The demand for funerals was too great to meet. The clergy wanted to care for the sick and dying and comfort the bereaved. Stanley, in particular, helped people to prepare their wills. There was also the need to bury the dead quickly to prevent further infection. Families buried their own dead in their gardens, and in the fields. Many graves were unmarked, or with only a small stone with a cross scratched on them as a memorial.

The second resolution of the village was to lock the church and to hold services in the open air in the natural amphitheatre of Cucklett Delph near to the village. This was to prevent the further spreading of disease between people. Mompesson held services in the Delph each week, preaching from a rock where he could see and be seen by everyone. An annual service of thanksgiving is held there on the last Sunday in August each year.

Holding services in the open air

And as a final resolution, the village resolved to place itself into quarantine. This would prevent the spread of the plague into the surrounding villages and towns, where the effect could have been devastating. The Earl of Devonshire arranged for food to be dropped at the boundary stone of the village. Other local villages provided bread and food. Money for these was placed in running water, to wash away the plague. On the boundary stone, where there was no running water, holes were drilled and filled with vinegar.

The Boundary Stone

The quarantine was very effective, and there were no deaths from plague in the surrounding area. The courage of the people of Eyam saved many. Inside the village, however, there were many personal tragedies. It is estimated that the total population of Eyam before the plague was about 800 people. Of them, 260 people died of plague, from 76 different families. Mompesson's wife Catherine, who had refused to leave at the start of the plague, was one of those who died. She had supported the resolution to quarantine the village, and shared in the work of visiting the sick and dying. She died on 23rd August 1666, aged 27. William wrote to his children and told them that 'your dear mother is now a saint in heaven'.

The final person to die, on 1st November 1666, was Abraham Morten, a farmworker. He was the eighteenth member of his family to die from the plague. About three weeks later, the quarantine was lifted and the process of recovery began. Mompesson urged that all the clothing and bedding in the village be burned. He burned his own possessions as an example, so that he wrote to his uncle saying that he had scarcely enough to clothe himself.

Although the Mompessons, William and Catherine, along with Thomas Stanley are those whose names feature prominently in this story, it is the whole village who are the saints. Together they resolved to enter into quarantine, to suffer and die together, and to save those who lived around them. At the heart of this decision was their faith in Jesus Christ. Not only were the people of Eyam following the teaching of Jesus, that, 'No one has greater love than this: to lay down their life for their friends' (John 15.13), they also embodied the pattern of Jesus' own life. Jesus died on the cross to bring healing and life to the world. The people of Eyam died, and lost their loved ones, to ensure the health and life of those around them. Their deep faith in God, and their trust that they had been saved already by the death and resurrection of Jesus, is what enabled this collective act of courage and sacrifice.

A Prayer for Pilgrims

God of life and death,

   we give you thanks for the people of Eyam,

   for their courage and their sacrifice,

   and for their faith in God.

May we follow in the way of Christ,

   having courage to reach out across divisions,

   and taking costly decisions to seek the health and wellbeing of

   others.

We pray for all who are affected by disease and pandemic today,

   that they might be restored to health,

   and find community among those who suffer with them.

We ask this in the name of Jesus,

   who died in order that we might live.

   Amen.

*'Ring o'roses': a wreath of roses is included in the commemorative window
in Eyam church, in reference to the nursery rhyme (Ring-a-ring-a-roses, a
pocket full of posies, atishoo, atishoo, we all fall down!). The Riley graves (of
the Hancock family who lived in a house in Riley Field) are shown below.*

Where to go

The village of Eyam is set in the Hope Valley, just off the A623 in the Peak District National Park.

The names of those who died are recorded all around the village. The parish church, S32 5QH has an illuminated copy of the register of deaths during the plague. A beautiful stained-glass window tells the story of the plague. The tomb of Catherine Mompesson stands outside in the churchyard, together with a monument to Thomas Stanley.

Eyam Museum, Hawkhill Road, S32 5QP includes the story of the plague years in some detail.

Further out from the centre of the village, it is worth the walk to find the boundary stone, Mompesson's Well and Cucklett Delph. Lovers Leap records one of the more tragic parts of the human story.

Also interesting

Plague Sunday:

The final Sunday of August is marked in Eyam as 'Plague Sunday'. A service of thanksgiving is held in Cucklett Delph, and red flowers are placed on Catherine Mompesson's tomb.

Peak Pilgrimage:

Eyam is one end of the Peak Pilgrimage (the other end is St Bertram's tomb at Ilam, see Chapter 5).

The pilgrimage trail was set up to mark the 350th anniversary of the plague, linking two villages afflicted by the plague. It is 39 miles long and the Ordnance Survey 1:25,000 map OL24 The Peak District - White Peak area covers the whole of the route.

The long distance walk is designed to be enjoyed by all. The route is almost entirely on footpaths through beautiful but easy walking countryside, popping into occasional villages and passing lots of pubs and cafes. There are a variety of accommodation options such B&B pubs, hotels, youth hostels, camping and caravan sites along the way, as well as a couple of Christian centres. Excursions to Chatsworth and other places off the main route can be planned in – including several places mentioned in this book.

Beginning at Ilam (see Chapter 5), it passes through Alstonefield, Hartington, Monyash (see Chapter 6), Over Haddon, Bakewell, Edensor and Chatsworth, Baslow, Curbar, Grindleford (see Chapter 7 with reference to the Padley Martyrs) and Stoney Middleton, finishing at Eyam.

Fuller details of the Peak Pilgrimage can be found at
www.peakpilgrimage.org.uk and a guidebook (with spaces for stamps
and stickers from churches along the route) can be ordered from
Eyam Parish Church.

There is also a newly planned Hope Walk route from Eyam, details
from the same website, which is 29 miles. Ordnance Survey 1:25,000
map OL1 The Peak District - Dark Peak area covers the whole of the
route.

10: The Reverend and Royal Astronomer:

John Flamsteed

Denby and Derby, 17th Century

John Flamsteed was born in Denby on 19th August 1646, to Stephen Flamsteed and Mary Spadman. John had a difficult childhood. His mother Mary died while he was young, and from the age of 14 he suffered from a chronic illness. He had arthritic knees and ankles, weak legs and frequent headaches which would affect him all his life.

John was educated at the free Derby School in St Peter's Churchyard in Derby, near to his father's malting business. John loved Latin, which was essential to read scientific papers, and excelled in history. He left school in 1662, but his ill-health delayed him going to Jesus College in Cambridge. Remaining in Derby, John helped in his father's business and developed his interests in mathematics and astronomy. He observed his first eclipse in the summer he left school, and by 1665 had written his first astronomical paper, including tables to calculate the latitude of Derby. He correctly predicted the solar eclipses of 22nd June 1666, and 25th October 1668. John eventually reached Cambridge in 1670, staying long enough to hear Sir Isaac Newton lecture, before leaving Cambridge to be ordained deacon in the Church of England.

John was on the verge of accepting a parish in Derbyshire when he was asked by King Charles II to advise a Royal Commission. The Commission was looking into some proposals by a French astronomer to use the position of the moon to establish longitude. Whilst rejecting this proposal as unhelpful, the Commission did recommend the establishment of an observatory and the appointment of an observer. So it was that the Revd John Flamsteed became the first Astronomer Royal – the King's Astronomical Observer – on 4th March 1672. His job was that of 'rectifieing the Tables of the motions of the Heavens, and the places of the fixed stars, so as to find out the so much desired Longitude of places for Perfecteing the Art of Navigation'. A warrant for the founding of the Royal Greenwich Observatory was issued in June 1672, and John Flamsteed laid the foundation stone on 10th August.

The following year, Flamsteed was made a Fellow of the Royal Society and moved into the newly completed observatory. He stayed there until 1684, when he left to be ordained priest and to take on the parish of Burstow in Sussex. He held both offices, Rector of Burstow and Astronomer Royal, until his death in 1719; he was buried in Burstow churchyard.

Flamsteed's achievements are many. He pioneered the systematic use of telescopic sights for his observations. He was the first person to record a sighting of Uranus, in December 1690, even if he mistook it for a star he called 34 Tauri. He invented a tool for map-making called 'conical projection' which allows spherical objects to be projected onto a flat plane – his method is still used today.

In November and December 1680, Flamsteed observed a comet passing towards and then away from the Sun in an elliptical orbit. He insisted it was a single comet, over the objections of Sir Isaac Newton and others who thought it was two comets. Flamsteed's argument would win Newton over eventually, and became the basis for Newton's account of the orbit of comets and planets.

This was not the only occasion on which Flamsteed and Newton were to fall out. Flamsteed and Newton were not easy men to deal with; neither found social interaction easy. In 1702, Newton persuaded Queen Anne to make him the Inspector to the Greenwich observatory, and therefore effectively Flamsteed's boss. Newton began to make a series of complaints that Flamsteed failed to follow his instructions. Flamsteed retaliated by complaining that Newton had not returned his books. Newton's own research needed Flamsteed's results and so Newton was impatient for Flamsteed to publish them. Flamsteed was a meticulous scientist and refused to publish his observations until he had checked and rechecked them. To this must be added his dislike of Newton, which meant he had no interest in publishing to help Newton's work. Newton, aided by Flamsteed's assistant Edmond Halley, stole Flamsteed's work in 1704, and published it against Flamsteed's wishes in 1712. Flamsteed spent a huge amount of money and managed to gather 300 of the 400 copies printed. He burned them all in a bonfire on Greenwich Park, which he described as 'as a sacrifice to heavenly truth'. Newton responded by removing all references to Flamsteed from his *Principia Mathematica*, despite the astronomer's huge contribution to the volume.

Only after his death were Flamsteed's great works published. His wife Margaret (who was also trained in mathematics and astronomy, and had worked closely with him) edited his catalogue of the stars, the *Historia Coelestis Britannica* of 1725, which identified 2935 stars. This was three times as many stars, and observed to a far greater degree of accuracy, than any earlier accounts (including the pirate copy of Flamsteed's work published by Newton and Halley). This was followed by the *Altas Coelestis* in 1729, charting the locations of the stars. Flamsteed's system of naming stars is still followed in part.

The Atlas Coelestis of 1729, a copy of which is owned by Derby Museum and Art Gallery. It is on display in the Museum of Making

It is no accident that because the Royal Observatory was sited in Greenwich, that place has become known as the basis for both time (Greenwich Mean Time) and space (the meridian passes through Greenwich). Nor is it a coincidence that Greenwich has a naval history. The interest in astronomy was linked very strongly with the use of the stars for navigation, and especially navigation at sea. This became crucial to trade and communication.

Christian faith has always rejected astrology – the telling of fortunes from the conjunction of the stars – but the Christian belief in an ordered creation, as evidenced through astronomy, the scientific study of celestial objects, is foundational to the origins of science. Flamsteed, who holds his head high among the beginnings of the scientific enlightenment, was a Christian priest. Although at this time there were many who wondered if scientific discoveries would overthrow faith, Flamsteed was a devout believer, and preached a noted sermon against atheism.

Flamsteed's scientific work, his observation and his patient, even painstaking, accuracy, were rooted in a deep faith in God. He believed that God had given him his gifts of scientific knowledge and aptitude. He even saw his physical frailty as part of God's provision for him. He wrote that, 'My desires have always been for learning and divinity: and though I have been accidentally put from it by God's providence, yet I have always thought myself more qualified for it than for any other employment; because my bodily weakness will not permit me action, and my mind has always been fitted for the contemplation of God and his works'. This vision of his work as the 'contemplation of God and his works' brought together Flamsteed's scientific work and his life of prayer and worship. For Flamsteed, the two belonged together.

A Prayer for Pilgrims

God of all space and time,

    we give you thanks for John Flamsteed,

    for his patient observation,

    and for his wonder at your creation.

May we follow in the way of Christ,

    taking time to enjoy the beauty of the universe,

    and seeing you at work in the order of creation.

We pray for all astronomers and scientists,

    that they might work together to increase our knowledge,

    and share their discoveries with all people.

We ask this in the name of Jesus,

    the Word who gives order to all creation.

    Amen.

'The heavens are telling the glory of God' (Ps 19):
the stellarsphere in Flamsteed Park, Denby

Where to go

Denby:

The John Flamsteed Memorial Park, DE5 8PG includes the Stellarsphere, a bronze and brass installation showing the position of stars in the sky overhead at the moment it is viewed.

Derby:

A copy of the *Historia Coelestis Britannica* is on display in the newly opened Museum of Making, DE1 3AF.

Flamsteed's school on St Peter's Churchyard, DE1 1NN is lost beneath the foundations of a more recent building. There is a blue plaque on his house at 28 Queens Street, DE1 3DL. He also has a star in the 'Made in Derby Walk of Fame' running from Albion Street, DE1 2PR to Exchange Street, DE1 2DU. Download the app, point it at the star and a virtual reality John Flamsteed will appear. More details at https://www.visitderby.co.uk/whats-on/made-in-derby-ii/.

Elsewhere in Derbyshire:

Flamsteed is commemorated in the John Flamsteed Community School in Denby; Flamsteed House at Ecclesbourne School in Duffield; the Flamsteed science block at John Port School in Derby; and a courtyard of residences at Derby University.

Further afield:

Pilgrims looking to venture further might like to know that there is a crater on the moon named Flamsteed, and that he has given his name to asteroid 4987 Flamsteed. Or you could simply explore Greenwich on your next visit to London, and look for Flamsteed House.

11. Scared into Sobriety:

Francis Brown and Halter Devil Chapel

Mugginton, Hulland Ward, 1723

It was a dark and stormy night, and Francis Brown had run out of drink. He had already consumed a great deal, but it wasn't enough. He had enough money, having stolen some from public funds. He decided to ride to Derby to drink in the pubs there. His wife tried to stop him, warning him that he had already had too much to drink. Francis, notorious for his heavy drinking, was determined. 'Ride I will, if I have to halter the Devil', he told her, and left the house.

Outside, in the mud and the dark, Francis stumbled towards the paddock. Try as he might he could not get the halter, the strap that goes around a horse's head and to which a rope is attached to lead it, over the head of his horse. Suddenly there was a great flash of lightning, and at the same time Francis received a strong blow. He fell to the ground unconscious.

His wife, hearing the commotion, came out and dragged her husband back inside. When he came round, he was terrified. In the lightning flash he had seen what he had been trying to put the harness on, and it had horns. 'It was the Devil', said Francis. 'I said I would halter the Devil, and that's what I was trying to do'. His wife disagreed. In his drunken state, Francis had been trying to put the halter on a cow, which had kicked him for its pains. But Francis remained fearful from his experience and would not change his story, however hard his wife tried to get him to see the truth.

Perhaps she didn't try very hard, because after his experience of trying to halter the Devil, Francis was a changed man. He gave up drinking, became an honest man and built a chapel for prayer attached to his farm. This was opened in 1723, and has always been known as the Halter Devil Chapel. When Francis died in 1731, he left instructions that the chapel should be left to the parish of Mugginton.

Halter Devil Chapel and adjoining farm

Francis is a saint who can tell us about our need for change. For Francis, this was sudden and came from fear. Others experience the change more slowly, but with no less effective a result. Whether sudden or gradual, change is something we all experience, and which we need if we are to find new and better ways of being.

A Prayer for Pilgrims

God of constancy and change,

    we give you thanks for Francis Brown,

    for the transformation that you brought to his life

    and for the chapel that he founded.

May we follow in the way of Christ,

    changing those parts of our lives that need it,

    and marking our new lives with imagination and generosity.

We pray for all who are addicted this day,

    that they may find the desire to seek help

    and know your power to change.

We ask this in the name of Jesus,

    who brought change to those he met.

    Amen.

The Horned Beast

Where to go

The Halter Devil Chapel stands on Intakes Lane between Hulland Ward and Mercaston (DE56 2LU). It is a rare example of a semi-detached chapel. Inside it is very small, about 13 by 14 feet (4 x 4.5m), and can hold about 30 people. In the 19th Century, it was used as a dairy by the neighbouring farm during the week. A panel, now destroyed, used to record its origins:

> *Francis Brown in his old age,*
>
> *did build him here an hermitage in 1723.*
>
> *Who being old and full of evil*
>
> *once on a time haltered the Devil.*

The registers of All Saints' Church in Mugginton, note that Francis Brown founded the 'Chappel in ye Intakes Hull'd Ward'.

Services are still held monthly in the Halter Devil Chapel, using ministry from All Saints' Church in Mugginton.

A key for the chapel may be available on request (see notices at the chapel, or https://www.achurchnearyou.com/church/13379/ for contact details).

12: Derby's Enlightenment:

John Whitehurst, Erasmus Darwin, Maria Jacson, Thomas Gisborne and Joseph Wright

Derby, Trusley, Dalbury, Matlock, Chesterfield, Somersal Herbert, Radbourne, Ashbourne, Breadsall, 18th-19th centuries

Eighteenth Century Derby was a place of learning and industry, part of a great wave of pioneering work in chemistry, physics, engineering and medicine powered by a passion for gathering, measuring, testing and communicating. We have already met one of the forerunners of the Enlightenment in John Flamsteed (Chapter 10).

In this chapter we concentrate on a few of the most well-known Derbyshire names; however, around 200 men and women across the Midlands were energetically pursuing similar goals, exchanging principles and practices, and applying their knowledge for tangible outcomes which promoted 'enlightenment' still further.

John Whitehurst

One of the greatest figures in Derby's Enlightenment was John Whitehurst (1713-1788). He was born in Cheshire and seems to have enjoyed exploring the Peak District as a boy. He was not formally educated, instead he followed in his father's business as a clockmaker. Whitehurst was fascinated by the business of clocks, which were some of the most innovative and important mechanical instruments of the time. He was also gifted at making clocks and other instruments. He moved to Derby in 1736 to set up his own business and was a great success. His most prominent works were the installation of the Town Hall clock, and both a clock and carillon in All Saints' Church (now Derby Cathedral). As well as clocks, Whitehurst made a range of precision instruments including thermometers, compasses and barometers. He gained a reputation as an engineer and was consulted widely in the town and county. He was also sought out to advise the mining industry, and he invented the 'pulsation engine', a device for raising water out of mines and the forerunner of the hydraulic ram.

Whitehurst married a Derbyshire woman, Elizabeth Gretton, the daughter of the Rector of Trusley and Dalbury in South Derbyshire. Elizabeth was a well-matched partner for Whitehurst, sharing his interests and correcting his published work when needed.

Whitehurst's house in Queen Street

In 1774, Whitehurst became Stamper of the Money Weights at the Royal Mint. This post came about at the recommendation of the Duke of Newcastle, for whom he had recently installed heating and plumbing. For the next five years Whitehurst divided his time between London and Derby, before moving permanently to the capital. He died in 1788, and was buried beside his wife in St Andrew's burial ground on Grays Inn Road.

Whitehurst's love of the Peak District and his work in mining came together in his work on geology. In 1763, he had written to Benjamin Franklin in America with some ideas for a 'General Theory of the Earth'. But it was not until 1778 that he published his *Inquiry into the Original State and Formation of the Earth*. This book was very much his life's work, and on its basis he was elected as a Fellow of the Royal Society in May 1779. He revised the work, and made significant additions, in 1786. A final edition of the work, showing some minor further amendments, was published in 1792, four years after his death.

Whitehurst's geological work is based primarily on his careful drawing and understanding of the strata of rocks in the Derwent valley and especially at Matlock. The second edition also includes drawings of Giant's Causeway in Ireland. Throughout the book he speaks both about the geology that he observes and at the same time he notes implications for his faith in God. It was geology that was the first challenge to the understanding of the Bible current at the time. Primate of All Ireland Archbishop Ussher (1581-1656) had dated the creation to 4004 BC by using biblical chronology. Yet the new science of geology suggested that the world was much, much older than that.

In his work, Whitehurst tries to compare geological findings with the creation stories in the book of Genesis.

Sketch from Whitehurst's geological drawings of the Matlock area

Most importantly, he tries to follow the scientific evidence, even when it challenges his theological assumptions.

Perhaps it is best to understand Whitehurst's *Inquiry* as a re-interpretation of the Bible through geological science. Whitehurst was a man of deep faith, Church Warden of All Saints' Church from 1761-62, and this work was challenging for him. But his honesty and determination to hold together geological understanding (God's creation) and the Bible (God's Word) is valuable, and points to an interaction of science and faith more productive than many other interpretations.

Erasmus Darwin

The inspirational ideas in this wave of scientific enquiry were exchanged in a number of ways: by correspondence, through writing books and papers, by speaking at meetings in people's houses, or simply by living or working in close proximity.

In 1758, Benjamin Franklin visited Matthew Boulton in Birmingham. Boulton had bought clock parts from Whitehurst, and the two shared a love of science. That same interest was shared between Boulton and Erasmus Darwin, who knew one another as some of Boulton's family were Darwin's patients. Franklin's visit brought all three together, with others, and the Lunar Society was formed. This was to remain an influential scientific society until the early 19th century.

Erasmus Darwin (1731-1802) was born in Nottinghamshire, and went to Chesterfield Grammar School where he developed interests in botany and poetry. These passions remained with him his entire life.

After university in Cambridge, Erasmus practiced medicine in Nottingham and then in Lichfield where he first settled. He married Mary Howard (known as Polly) and they lived in the Cathedral close, where their five children were born, of whom two died in infancy.

After Polly's death, Erasmus fathered two children by a servant, Mary Parker. He later bought a pub in Ashbourne which these two daughters, the Misses Parker, ran as a girls' school. Erasmus supported them further in this enterprise by writing *A Plan for the Conduct of Female Education in Boarding Schools*. This was radical for its time, and included recommendations that girls learn science and visit factories.

On his appointment as physician to the Pole family of Radbourne Hall, Erasmus fell in love with Elizabeth, the wife of Colonel Pole. When Pole died five years later, it was Erasmus who waited in Radbourne Church to marry the most eligible widow in Derbyshire. Elizabeth refused to move to Lichfield, so Erasmus moved to Radbourne.

In 1782, Erasmus and Elizabeth moved again, to Full Street in Derby. Erasmus set up his medical practice there, which he expanded to include a dispensary for the sick poor of the town. However, he greatly missed the Lunar Society meetings when he moved, and the relocation to Derby prompted him to form the Derby Philosophical Society, which would become another learned scientific society that would extend the Midlands network of scientific understanding across the world.

Erasmus continued his scientific interests and published his major works. These included *Zoonomia*, which suggested that all life could be descended from 'a single living filament'. This is perhaps the earliest account of a theory of evolution, which Erasmus' grandson Charles would make famous. He presented his evolutionary ideas in verse, in particular the posthumously published poem *The Temple of Nature*, and was an influence on Wordsworth and Coleridge.

'Am I Not A Man And A Brother?' Wedgwood's anti-slavery medal

Erasmus' poems made public his opposition to the slave trade. He became friends with other abolitionists, not least Josiah Wedgwood. Towards the end of his life, Erasmus wrote about the sugar plant, and included this plea: "Great God of Justice! grant that it may soon be cultivated only by the hands of freedom".

In 1802, the Darwins moved to Breadsall Priory. This had been left to Erasmus by his son, who committed suicide in 1799. The tragedy was compounded when within weeks of the move, Erasmus died suddenly, probably due to a lung infection. He was buried in Breadsall parish church.

The death of Erasmus Darwin left a gap that was hard to fill. His enthusiasm and remarkably wide interests had been the energy driving the Derby Philosophical Society; nevertheless, after his death the members continued to meet and arrange lectures.

The membership included many familiar names – Josiah Wedgwood and other members of the Wedgwood family; porcelain designer William Duesbery who developed what became Crown Derby; and the mill owning Strutts (who we shall meet again in chapter 14). It was a very grounded gathering of manufacturers who were keen to learn all they could about the new sciences. Their discussions were not limited to science, but included some of the most thought provoking works of the time on politics and economics, including Adam Smith's 'Wealth of Nations' and John Howard's book on prison reform 'The State of the Prisons'.

Perhaps its most important legacy was that the library of books so carefully selected by the members was bequeathed to the Derby Central Library.

Erasmus Darwin was a polymath, a man of many talents and interests. His most notable contributions were to biology, medicine, education, engineering, poetry, and the abolition of slavery, but there is much more that could be written about him. In an account of saints, Erasmus' care for the poor and the enslaved is especially important. His scientific work brought him into conflict with some in the church and the religious establishment. His views at times seem near to Deism, the belief that God began the universe and then left it alone. But he was known to be a faithful church-goer at All Saints in Derby. Like his friend John Whitehurst, and others in his circle such as Maria Jacson, Erasmus Darwin knew the tension that scientific advances brought to traditional Christian faith.

Maria Jacson

While still in Lichfield, Erasmus had developed a prominent reputation as a doctor. He treated Georgiana, Duchess of Devonshire with electric shocks to try and restore the sight in her eye (it was not successful). Georgiana was very curious about all the latest scientific enquiries, and occasionally participated in soirées and discussions, both in Derbyshire and at the Royal Society in London.

While it would be relatively easy for a high-born lady to participate in the exciting scientific discussions of the time, it was more difficult for a woman of the middle classes. She would have to battle against the prevailing opinion that sewing and the art of polite conversation were the most appropriate pursuits for young ladies – despite (or perhaps because of) the radical ideas emanating from the French Revolution, and from the Rational Dissenters such as Mary Wollstonecraft. They believed in the primacy of reason in tandem with scripture, and that education was the key to women's liberation.

One Derbyshire resident caught up in this debate was Maria Jacson (1755-1829). As a young adult, she was greatly admired by Erasmus Darwin, who praised her skill as a botanist and botanical artist. But life would lead her into a debate as fierce as the one between science and the bible: the strictures on girls' education and women's proper place in society.

Maria was born in Cheshire, but moved to Somersal Herbert, Derbyshire, after the death of her clergyman father, whom she had been nursing. Now in her forties, her fortunes changed, and she and her sister were required to write for a living while trying to pay off the recurring debts of her brother, also a clergyman, who had taken to drink and gambling.

Her series of books combine research on plant propagation, Linnaean classification and the techniques of dissection, with practical guides to cultivation and garden design. *Botanical Dialogues Between Hortensia and her Four Children, Charles, Harriet, Juliette and Henry Designed For the Use in Schools (1797)* is constructed around conversations between a mother and her children, including the different social roles that her sons and daughters are destined to fulfil in society on account of their gender. Nevertheless, while outlining the social norms, she is also at pains to distance herself from them.

Her principal readers were women and children, who were typically excluded from access to 18th century scientific writing, and her aim was to engage: 'to induce even a few of my sister Florists to exercise their intellect, or relieve their ennui' through 'the study of vegetable existence'.

Unsurprisingly, she provoked a backlash against educated women ('unsex'd females') and stirred up moral concerns, such as whether the delicate matter of the sexual reproduction of plants was appropriate matter for 'female modesty'.

Nevertheless, throughout these books Maria quietly (and sometimes bitterly) adds to the contemporary discussion about the proper education of women, and the ways in which they should not passively submit but actively extend their sphere of activity, and build a society where a woman could 'be a self for herself and her God, rather than for her husband'.

Thomas Gisborne

Another of Erasmus Darwin's many patients was Thomas Gisborne (1758-1846). Thomas was born on Bridge Gate in Derby and later revived his links with the town both as a benefactor, including initiating the building of the Derby Infirmary (see Chapter 14) and as a patron, commissioning the architect Joseph Pickford to build him St Helen's House in the new Palladian style. He was also a founder member of the Derby Philosophical Society.

After an education at Harrow and Cambridge, he was ordained to the parish of Barton-under-Needwood in Staffordshire in 1783. He married, and also inherited the nearby Yoxall Lodge. One of his abiding passions was botany, and he held the post of professor at

Cambridge at the same time as being vicar to his parish. His collection of 600 species was later preserved by the British Museum.

Having met William Wilberforce in Cambridge, Gisborne became a central figure in the Clapham Sect. This was a group of evangelical Christians who campaigned for the abolition of the slave trade, and Thomas published *Remarks Respecting the Abolition of the Slave Trade* in 1792. Wilberforce was a frequent visitor to Yoxall Lodge, which became a focus for the group.

Thomas Gisborne is often referred to in memorials and biographies as a poet: *Poems Sacred and Moral* (1798) was a selection he wrote alongside his other creative psalms and hymns, and the serene *Walks in a Forest* (1794) showed his passion for the woodland estate around his home. However, his more influential and controversial works include *Principles of Moral Philosophy* (1789), and *An Enquiry into the Duties of the Female Sex* (1797), which was referenced by none other than Jane Austen. His *Considerations on Modern Theories of Geology (1837)* is very critical of the findings of geology where they depart from scripture.

Recognised as a man who combined his faith, talents and wealth to help the causes he was passionate about, it would have been very interesting to hear him discuss some of these topics with others in this chapter!

Joseph Wright

The final figure for this chapter on Derby's Enlightenment is Joseph Wright (1734-97). Joseph was also a patient of Erasmus Darwin, and like Darwin binds many of the Enlightenment saints together because he painted their portraits and even some of their experiments. While several of these hang in the Joseph Wright gallery in Derby Museum, the fine and sensitive paintings of Thomas Gisborne and his wife Mary and of the Pickfords are elsewhere.

Born in Irongate in Derby, Joseph enjoyed visiting workshops as a child, and was fascinated by watching craftsmen at work. He was also a musician, playing the flute with friends, including the organist of All Saints' Church on Irongate. Although All Saints was where he worshipped, he was actually baptised in St Michael's Church nearby and buried in St Alkmund's Church (now demolished).

In his paintings, Joseph used chiaroscuro, which emphasises light and dark, to great effect. His work as a painter of portraits and landscapes is superb, but it is in his paintings of industrial and scientific scenes that we really mark his greatness.

One of his most famous paintings is *A Philosopher Lecturing on the Orrery* (1764-66). Not only has he accurately understood the subject matter of the lecture, but he also shows the faces of the audience illuminated by the experiment being demonstrated. They are caught, literally, in the moment of being enlightened.

The Enlightenment is often seen as a movement away from faith to the light of reason, but the saints of Derby's Enlightenment reveal a more complex picture.

John Whitehurst and Erasmus Darwin show us different aspects of the way in which honest seeking after truth was both a scientific and a religious virtue. Maria Jacson illustrates how advances in one field – botany – could demonstrate the equal importance of both male and female attributes, and thereby influence debate about society's suppression of women. She influenced access to education for girls, and the honouring of women's capacity to engage in scientific endeavour. Thomas Gisborne's repudiation of the science of geology is out of step with the others. However, his campaigning against the slave trade was shared with Darwin and demonstrates an ethical enlightenment for which he is rightly remembered. And finally, Joseph Wright's paintings seem to show the spiritual joy of the Enlightenment's insights into the intricacies of creation.

A Prayer for Pilgrims

God of light and darkness,

we give you thanks for John Whitehurst, Erasmus Darwin, Maria

Jacson, Thomas Gisborne and Joseph Wright,

for their commitment to truth

and for their work to end slavery and subjugation.

May we follow in the way of Christ

seeking truth with honesty and courage,

and working to free those enslaved and oppressed today.

We pray for all who are trapped in modern forms of slavery,

that they may find freedom and liberation,

and be healed from trauma.

We ask this in the name of Jesus,

who spoke the truth and brought freedom to captives.

Amen

*The armillary sphere atop Joseph Wright's monument outside his birthplace
in Irongate, Derby.*

Where to go

A number of places in Derby bring together the figures of Derby's Enlightenment, and there are several blue plaques throughout the city which commemorate its leading figures.

Derby Cathedral:

Derby Cathedral, formerly All Saints' Church on Irongate, DE1 3GP is where John Whitehurst was Church Warden and where Erasmus Darwin and Joseph Wright worshipped.

In the Cavendish Area to the right of the main altar, Joseph Wright's simple tombstone has found a resting place following the demolition of St Alkmund's Church in the 1960s.

Outside the Cathedral:

A memorial to John Whitehurst can be found in the pavement opposite the west door of the Cathedral, and a blue plaque marks the location of John Whitehurst's clock works at 28 Queen Street, DE1 3DL.

Joseph Wright's birthplace at 28 Irongate, DE1 3GA is marked by an elaborate monument, with a representation of an armillary sphere. There is also a blue plaque at his home at 28 Queen Street DE1 3DL, which was previously also the home of John Flamsteed (see Chapter 10).

Wright also has a star in the 'Made in Derby Walk of Fame' running from Albion Street (DE1 2PR) to Exchange Street (DE1 2DU). Download the app, point it at the star and a virtual reality Joseph

Wright will appear. More details at
https://www.visitderby.co.uk/whats-on/made-in-derby.

Erasmus Darwin's Derby house on Full Street, DE1 3AF has a plaque, and there is a further memorial to him on Exeter Bridge, DE1 2ED.

Finally, there is a plaque to Thomas Gisborne on St Helens' House by Bridge Gate, DE1 3EE, jointly with William Strutt, who we shall meet in the next chapter.

Derby Museum and Art Gallery:

The Museum and Art Gallery (DE1 1BS) has a whole room devoted to Joseph Wright's paintings, including *A Philosopher Lecturing on the Orrery*, together with his portrait of Erasmus Darwin and other notables of the time, and some self-portraits.

Elsewhere in the museum, there is a bust of Erasmus Darwin and a small display about him.

Derby Museum of Making:

Derby's iconic Silk Mill, DE1 3AF is part of the UNESCO World Heritage Derwent Trail, and has now reopened as the Museum of Making celebrating 300 years of Derby innovation and engineering. A number of exhibits relating to the Enlightenment are on display – such as Erasmus Darwin's microscope and some of his writings.

Derby Central Library:

The books collected by the Derby Philosophical Society were bequeathed to the library and are now in the archives of the Local Studies Centre, DE1 2FS.

Elsewhere around Derbyshire:

Erasmus Darwin's school in Chesterfield still stands. It is now a campus of Chesterfield College, S41 7LL. St Andrew's Church in Radbourne, DE6 4LY, where Erasmus married for the second time, is worth a visit. Erasmus' burial place is marked by a memorial in Breadsall parish church, DE21 5LA.

The school in Ashbourne which was run by Erasmus' daughters, the Misses Parker, can be seen at DE6 1GH. Formerly the Old Nags Head Inn, it is now known as Madge House. There is a plaque on the exterior wall. Inside it is now apartments.

Somersal Herbert Hall, DE6 5PD where Maria Jacson lived and worked, is privately owned. Its timber-framed front is unusual in Derbyshire.

Somersal Herbert Hall

Also interesting

The Cathedral clock:

The clock on the Cathedral tower stills contains evidence of repair work which John Whitehurst carried out in 1745. Repair work in 1964 confirmed a long-standing rumour concerning his repurposing of some armaments: Bonnie Prince Charlie's army had stayed in Derby in 1745, and Whitehurst had needed two long tubes to support and operate the clock hands, for which he used the gun barrels from discarded carbines. They are still in place.

The current clock was made by Smith of Derby, a company founded by one of Whitehurst's apprentices, to mark the church becoming a cathedral in 1927.

The Quad:

When passing the Quad Arts Centre in the Market Square in Derby, DE1 3AS, pause to wonder if the architect was inspired by John Whitehurst's geological studies, which were fundamental to the industrial development of the Derwent and Derby.

Orreries and Armillary Spheres:

Joseph Wright's memorial in Irongate is often referred to as an orrery, but is in fact an armillary sphere, which is a fixed model consisting of a spherical framework of rings, centred on Earth or the Sun. The rings represent lines of celestial longitude and latitude and other astronomically important features.

An orrery is a mechanical model of the Solar System that illustrates or predicts the relative positions and motions of the planets and moons.

Orreries usually consist of a globe in the centre and a series of arms with models of the planets (and maybe their moons) which can move round the central globe. They are typically driven by a clockwork mechanism.

The orrery was also known as a planetarium, though in modern usage the word usually refers to a domed auditorium where the movements of stars and planets are projected onto the inside of the dome.

The first orrery or planetarium of the modern era was produced in 1704. One was presented to Charles Boyle, 4th Earl of Orrery – hence the name.

13. Pubs, Pulpits and Preachers:

John Hieron and Joseph Hollingworth

Breadsall, Dale Abbey, Derby, 17th-19th centuries

Dale Abbey church

In addition to a hermitage and a ruined abbey, the village of Dale Abbey has a unique church. It was originally built by Cornelius, the hermit of Depedale (see Chapter 6), and then developed as the infirmary and the chapel to Dale Abbey. There was a connecting door to allow patients to access the chapel without going outside. After the dissolution of the monasteries in 1539, the chapel was taken over as the village church and the infirmary became a farmhouse, and then later still the Blue Bell Inn. The front bar was used by clergy to robe before taking services, entering the church through the connecting door. The door was also used in reverse, with members of the congregation leaving services to find refreshment in the bar.

The two characters in this chapter are separated by a hundred years, and they continue Dale Abbey's story of being a haven for deeply committed faithfulness.

John Hieron

The Revd John Hieron's activities in Dale Abbey began with a monthly 'lecture' or sermon during the 1640s, while he was Rector of Breadsall. The journey which brought him there is another tale of entanglement with the political and religious upheavals of the times.

John was born in August 1608 in Stapenhill, where his father was minister, and educated in Repton. He was ordained to Egginton in 1630, from where he preached at Newton Solney and established a weekly lecture at Bretby at the invitation of Countess Catherine of Chesterfield. He then moved to Ashbourne with the title of 'Lecturer'.

While in Ashbourne, John got into trouble for the content of his sermons and was summoned to Lambeth to answer for them to the Archbishop of Canterbury. The nature of the complaint is not known, but he managed to continue in Ashbourne until the Civil War broke out (1642-51), at which point, as he was a puritan and parliamentarian, he fled to Derby.

In 1644, he became Rector of Breadsall, and it was from Breadsall that he began to preach in Dale Abbey. His sermons became an important feature of life in the village. They were well attended and had an impact on the lives of those who heard. He was known as 'very zealous for God, earnest in every part of his work, and very compassionate in dealing with troubled souls'. He was a puritan, and his sermons urged his hearers to allow their whole lives to be transformed by their faith. An important part of this was observing the Sabbath, and he preached against the whole variety of sports and activities that took place on Sundays.

John Hieron's lectures in Dale Abbey continued until 1662. With the restoration of the monarchy, ministers in the Church of England had to conform to the use of the new Book of Common Prayer and to swear allegiance to the king. John refused to do so. He said he would 'Rather lose all than sin against God. If Breadsall parsonage was the best bishopric in England, I must do again what I have done'. Even after he had been ejected from Breadsall, he petitioned the bishop to allow him to continue his monthly lecture in Dale Abbey. The bishop refused unless he conformed.

John moved on, first to Little Eaton, and then to Loscoe. He continued to preach, mostly in homes and small gatherings to avoid the attention of the authorities. This, coupled with writing books of sermons, and *Remarks upon Scripture* enabled him to continue his ministry until he died, aged 73, on 6th July 1682.

The Methodist Society

The ejection of John Hieron left Dale Abbey to the more formal religion of the established church. Then in 1771, an itinerant preacher called Mr Bardsley came to Dale Abbey. He was a Methodist and after his visit a Methodist Society was formed in the village.

The line between John Hieron's lectures and the Methodist Society is broken, but real: the people of Dale Abbey responded to good Gospel-based preaching, and one hundred years after John Hieron had died, this Methodist Society in Dale Abbey produced one of the great Methodist preachers of the early 19th Century, Joseph Hollingworth.

Joseph Hollingworth

The Hollingworth family were long established in Dale Abbey. They were the publicans of the Blue Bell Inn, which adjoined the church. Joseph's grandfather, William Hollingworth, had been one of the founder members of the Dale Abbey Methodist Society, and his parents had been influenced by that society and by the Moravian community in Ockbrook.

Born at Dale Abbey in November 1781, Joseph Hollingworth grew up in a family of devout Methodists, but he himself, however, was not particularly interested in matters of faith as a young man. He teased his sister Elizabeth when she professed a personal faith. But when Elizabeth died, the day after Whitsun in 1805, Joseph was changed. On her deathbed, Elizabeth urged Joseph to prepare for his own death. This cut through his cynicism and left him anxiously examining himself and seeking after God. Joseph came to trust in the death of Jesus as the source of forgiveness for his sins and found joy and peace in this. He became a devout Methodist.

It was not long before Joseph, encouraged by one of his father's labourers, William Bacon, was teaching the Bible to others in the village. In 1807, he became a Local Preacher and went to other villages to preach and teach. The following year, he was called by the Methodist Conference, which was meeting in Bristol, to a full-time ministry of preaching. On Sunday 21st August 1808, Joseph preached three times in his father's barn in Dale Abbey to large congregations. 'My heart was full of love to Him, and of zeal to promote his glory. May I be faithful unto death', he told them.

Joseph became an itinerant preacher, based in one place but travelling the surrounding area, known as a 'circuit'. His letters tell of preaching in Durham, Sunderland and Nottingham, and of conversions, both dramatic and quiet. He was a faithful preacher, who spoke plainly to people about God and Jesus Christ. The letters also speak of him returning to Dale Abbey from time to time and preaching there. He was stationed twice in the Derby circuit. During his first stay, 1820-23, his father and his daughter Priscilla died. By the time he returned to the Derby circuit in 1835, he was a widower and was ill and near death himself. Before entering the chapel in King Street in Derby to preach he said, 'I believe this will be the last time I shall ever enter that pulpit'. The congregation watched him struggle to climb the pulpit steps, he was so weak, but once he began to preach, he became animated and lively. He warned them, as a dying man, to prepare for death and eternity. His final sermon thus echoed his sister's urging on her deathbed, which had first propelled Joseph into faith and preaching. Joseph died on 26th January 1836 at the age of 55.

Both John Hieron and Joseph Hollingworth show us the power of preaching to connect with people's lives and hearts. Both lived as they preached, taking care to be faithful to God and to back up their words in the pulpit with integrity and compassion in their daily lives. For both, Christian faith was rooted in the death of Jesus which enables forgiveness from sins and the transformation of individual lives.

A Prayer for Pilgrims

God who changes lives,

    we give you thanks for John Hieron and Joseph Hollingworth,

    for their passion in preaching your love for all people,

    and for their integrity in living out their words.

May we follow in the way of Christ

    showing others the path of life and love,

    and offering care to those in need.

We pray for all who preach today,

    that they might match their words with lives that point to you

    and care for all whom they teach.

We ask this in the name of Jesus,

    who preached to many, with his words and his deeds.

    Amen

'We preach Christ Crucified' (1 Corinthians 1:23). The font in All Saints'
Church, originally in Dale Abbey itself.

Where to go

John Hieron

Dale Abbey:

The key to All Saints' Church, DE7 4QA is held in one of the houses in the village: a noticeboard on the edge of the churchyard gives details.

The church is a fantastic space and contains the font from the Abbey, dating from around 1450. The pulpit in the church leans a little, and is dated 1634, so it is likely that John Hieron used it for his lectures and preaching. In the church you can see the bricked-up doorway that once led into the Blue Bell Inn. What was the Inn is now a private residence, and visitors need to respect the privacy of those living there. Outside in the churchyard many of the gravestones record the lives and faith of the Hollingworth family. Some of the gravestones have unusual carvings – the local stonemason must have had a lively imagination!

Elsewhere:

John Hieron's life can be traced through a number of Derbyshire churches. Stapenhill, DE15 9AF where his father was minister and where John was born; Egginton, DE65 6HS, which was the church to which John was ordained; Newton Solney, DE15 0SR where he preached; Bretby DE15 0QR where he established a Lecture; Ashbourne, DE6 1AN where he was appointed as Lecturer; and Breadsall, DE21 5LA where he was Rector and from where he established the Dale Abbey lecture.

Joseph Hollingworth

The King Street Methodist Chapel in Derby, DE1 3DZ with the pulpit in which Joseph Hollingworth preached his final sermon, was rebuilt in 1840 to accommodate more people. The new chapel was demolished in 1966.

Carving on one of the gravestones in Dale Abbey churchyard

Also interesting

Parts of the ruined Dale Abbey itself were distributed around the area, when the Act of Dissolution in 1539 brought an end to almost four centuries of monastic life in the Dale. Only the bare bones of the 40-foot-high chancel window remain. Excavations have shown the church to have possessed transepts 100 feet in length, a crossing tower, a cloister 85 feet square and a nave of unknown length.

The furnishings and fittings were either gradually sold off or stripped out and installed in other churches. Morley Church became home to some of the stained and painted glass, floor tiles and an entire porchway. The ornately carved font cover was installed in Radbourne Church, while Chaddesden received a window frame. The font eventually found its way back to All Saints' Church in Dale Abbey in 1884, and the slabs upon which the canons walked for so many centuries can be found in the grounds of the church at the Moravian Settlement at Ockbrook. It is thought that the tenor bell of Derby Cathedral originally belonged to Dale Abbey.

14: Benevolent Dispositions:

Jedediah Strutt, William Strutt and Joseph Strutt

South Normanton, Findern, Cromford, Derby, Belper, Milford, 18th-19th centuries

Our next story takes us to Derby on 16th September 1840: the opening of one of Britain's first and most influential urban public parks, Derby Arboretum, with a grand parade from the Market Place, a three-day holiday for workers, and more than 20,000 visitors gathered among the newly planted trees to hear the civic speeches and await the launch of a balloon.

Concluding his address, the donor of this landmark amenity, twice mayor Joseph Strutt said: 'It would be ungrateful in me not to employ a portion of the fortune which I possess, in promoting the welfare of those amongst whom I live, and by whose industry I have been aided in its acquisition'.

A noted philanthropist from a staunchly non-conformist background, Joseph Strutt was grateful to the working people of Derby for the part they had played in helping him and his family amass their fortune. He wanted to convey his thanks by giving the people a place where they could exercise and relax in the rapidly expanding and urbanising town.

Derby Arboretum featured more than 1,000 different species of trees and shrubs, and was specifically created for the public to educate themselves about botany and the glory of God's creation. Admission was free on Sundays and Wednesdays (which had been adopted as half day closing in Derby) which meant that working people, who had limited time and probably lacked the means to pay admission, could gain free access to the Arboretum when they had time off.

So how had Joseph and his family amassed their fortune? And what inspired their notable civic philanthropy?

No-one travelling along the Derwent Valley can fail to notice the dominance of mills, or indeed that it is a UNESCO World Heritage site. This is because, for a brief moment in history, the 15 mile stretch of the Derwent Valley from Matlock Bath to Derby was the most industrialised place on the planet. The wind of change which had inspired the Enlightenment (described in Chapter 12), with its restless curiosity, scientific investigations and practical applications into mechanics and engineering, also drove Derbyshire's mill developments. By the early 1720s the River Derwent itself was already providing power for John Lombe's innovative Silk Mill in Derby and would now be harnessed to power the mills of Matlock Bath, Cromford, Belper, Milford and Darley Abbey. The development from water to steam power would lead the industrial revolution, and though it would find its greatest centres elsewhere, it was based upon the innovations in technology and industry that began in Derby and the Derwent Valley.

Many of the principal players in this revolution had been excluded from the traditional classics-based university education of Oxford and Cambridge because they came from Dissenting families – though as their prosperity increased some joined the Church of England to place themselves closer to being gentry. Nevertheless, their discussions tended towards free-ranging philosophical examination of every aspect of life. Freed from conventional attitudes and the complacent religious conservatism of the landed gentry, they questioned even the belief in the Trinity, preferring a simple belief in the unity of God.

The view that Sunday readings and prayers and preaching were meaningless without action was at the heart of their faith, an attitude which drew in not only Charles Dickens, but also radical reformers and philosophers Mary Wollstonecraft and Joseph Priestley, writer Elizabeth Gaskell, innovators and inventors Josiah Wedgwood and Erasmus Darwin, among many others. They affirmed the essential unity of humankind and of creation, standing for tolerance, inclusivity, reason and social justice, including the abolition of slavery, and believed that the possession of wealth brought responsibility.

Jedediah Strutt (1726-1797)

We met Joseph's father Jedediah Strutt briefly in Chapter 12. He was a prodigious inventor and industrial organiser. Born in 1726, he was the second of the three sons of William Strutt, a small tenant farmer and maltster of Newton Old Hall, South Normanton near Alfreton. William was a severe man who took little interest in his sons, but Jedediah showed an early aptitude for mechanics and was apprenticed to a wheelwright in Findern when he was 14, where he lodged with the Woolatt family, who were hosiers. Some years later, in 1755, he married their daughter Elizabeth.

Findern was distant enough from Derby to have one of the largest Dissenting academies in the country, with theology that was liberal and influential among the working people. (At that time the law decreed that no Dissenting meeting house should be within five miles from the nearest town.) Its teaching included modern languages, modern history, politics, mathematics and natural philosophy (i.e. science). This curriculum and the spirit of discussion and enquiry were in tune with the experience and aspirations of the workers, and Jedediah was attracted to their cool rationalism and liberal thinking.

He was serious minded and introspective, with great mechanical aptitude, and Elizabeth supplied the drive for him to turn from farming to embark on his new career as an inventor and engineer. Working in partnership with his brother-in-law William Woolatt and various others in the hosiery business, he began by improving the Elizabethan-era stocking frame. He invented a process for making ribbed stockings by machine, the Derby Rib Machine, and applied for patents in 1758 and 1759.

When they moved to Derby, the Strutts formed friendships among the Presbyterian congregation meeting at Friargate chapel, of which Jedediah became a trustee from 1778. Their friends included the Duesburys of the china works, some Non-conformist ministers and their families, and fellow venturers in hosiery and cotton spinning. Jedediah poured out his thoughts on paper and was proud of his growing success as a hosier. In a letter to Elizabeth he wrote about how important it was 'early to improve ones mind in every moral ..... & useful improvement' in the hope to 'not only help to replenish the world, but be useful in it' and 'by all honest means' not only to provide for family and others by a life of 'diligence, honesty, sobriety & virtue; [but also] to have been the Author of anything great or good whereby mankind are made wiser or better'.

Their home life was quite frugal and the younger Strutts were constantly encouraged in self-reliance and industry.

By 1769, Jedediah was established and prosperous and working with Richard Arkwright (1732-92). They were two of a group of entrepreneurs who developed the country's textile industry, which eventually embraced all fibres both natural and manmade They built mills along the Derwent Valley from Derby to Matlock Bath. Together they founded the world's first water powered cotton spinning mill at Cromford, to a design inspired by the huge water wheel powering a number of factory processes at the Derby Silk Mill. They built on land owned by Peter Nightingale (great-uncle of Florence, who we shall meet in Chapter 16) and used water power from a reliable stream which flowed from the lead mines at Bonsall, near Wirksworth, and which never froze.

When Jedediah Strutt and Richard Arkwright began the construction at Cromford, partly on the site of a medieval corn mill, there was no village or labour force to hand. Cromford was remote, with none of the roads we have now - the A6 valley road was not built until 1820 - so it was reached over the moorland. A village had to be built, as well as weirs, dams, machine shops, roads and bridges, truckshops, and much more. These attracted skilled labour to the remote location, and once settled, the workers were held there by the arts of industrial incentive: hard work and strict rules, but with pecuniary and material rewards, celebrations, balls and holidays. It is notable that whereas there was rioting and destruction in some of the Lancashire mills, led by groups concerned that industrialisation would put them out of work, Cromford was not affected.

The Cromford factory village became one of the 'Wonders of the Peak', and visitors taking the waters at the spa towns of Matlock and Buxton would come to marvel. This integrated community of mills, chapels and Sunday schools, markets and inns, with decent housing, and all in stone and brick, was a full philanthropic package established entirely without assistance from the state or any local authority, and with no already existing public services.

In contrast, when Jedediah began a 40-year development of mills at Belper and Milford from 1777, independently of Arkwright, he attracted his labour force from existing cottage industries in these small towns. The older part of Belper was at that time a hamlet of framework knitters and nail makers, but had a market place, ale houses, shops and a chapel.

Once Jedediah had secured land for the new mills, the first of which opened in 1778, he prioritised the building of the Unitarian chapel and demonstrated his belief in toleration by assisting other denominations also to provide places of worship – sometimes giving financial help or a gift of land. In time there would be eight Strutt mills at Belper which would grow to a population of 10,000 by the mid-nineteenth century and be the second largest town in the county.

In 1781, he bought the old forge at Makeney by Milford Bridge, and Hopping Mill Meadow, a site which already included a fulling and dyeing mill. He opened his first mill there in 1782. The final complex included spinning, bleaching and dyeing mills, printers, foundries, joiners' workshops, a gas-works and a corn-mill.

The Unitarian Chapel in Belper

Jedediah died on 7th May 1797 and was buried in the Unitarian chapel in Belper. The affairs of the Strutt enterprise were already in the hands of his three sons who took on different areas of responsibility.

Of the three, middle son George Benson Strutt (1761-1841) was most intimately concerned with continuing the work of his father in ensuring that the workforce had adequate housing as well as arranging supplies of provisions for the growing populations around the mills.

Feeding the workforce was a concern, so the family established a dairy and agreed to buy sufficient qualities of milk to make it worthwhile to keep the cows through the winter. Profits from some of the provisioning enterprises paid for medical care, and they established a sick club. The Belper Provision Company was a cooperative enterprise distributing its profits among its customers in proportion to the value of their purchases.

Education was available through schools and Sunday schools, and places of worship were also provided and supported. George was prominent in local Belper affairs including the Belper Bank for Savings. His great grandson donated the Belper River Gardens in 1904, a school in 1909, public baths including a swimming pool in 1910 and the Belper Memorial Gardens in 1922.

George's memorial is with his father's in the Unitarian chapel in Belper.

William Strutt (1756-1830)

Eldest son William was interested in the design and construction of fireproof buildings and hot air systems. He built mills (and rebuilt if necessary) to protect them from the spread of fire. He also designed some of the houses and farms sustaining the workforce. Following his *tour de force*, the Derbyshire General Infirmary, he became known for the design of hospitals nationwide.

In Derby he is remembered for civic improvements to paving, lighting, bridges, the gas works, flood defences and educational establishments, though he attracted controversy for enclosing Nun's Green to pay for these improvements. He was made a Freeman and Burgess of the borough, which allowed him to vote in parliament. He was also a Deputy Lieutenant of Derbyshire, and was elected as a Fellow of the Royal Society, amongst other achievements.

Through his friendship with Erasmus Darwin, William had access to members of the Lunar Society, and he was a founder member (and president for 28 years) of the Derby Philosophical Society. He corresponded with scholars on mathematical, theoretical and practical problems, and with influential literary figures such as Coleridge and Southey, the Benthams and Robert Owen, who wrote of William and his brother Joseph as being among 'men of great practical knowledge …. whose talent in various ways and whose truly benevolent dispositions have seldom been equalled'.

William died on 9th December 1830, and his obituary notice recalled the many inventive and inspiring benefits he had brought to the town, with 'no motive than the public advantage'.

Derbyshire General Infirmary

Joseph Strutt (1765-1844)

Youngest son Joseph, as we have seen, was actively involved in Derby affairs, especially in education, and is chiefly remembered locally for his gift of the Arboretum. He was a lifelong radical social reformer and dedicated the majority of his time in the service of the town. He held the firm conviction that in order to gain the respect of the working classes and raise their education and aspirations, they must be allowed the same opportunities to enjoy civilized pleasures, such as art exhibitions and open spaces, as enjoyed by the upper classes.

With his nephew Edward he founded Derby's Mechanics' Institution, and opened his own house, with its paintings and statues, to the public. He was the first mayor to take office after the reform of the borough in 1835. He died on 13th January 1844, at his home in St. Peter's Street, after attending a meeting to cast his vote in favour of improving Derby's sanitary conditions. He and his wife Isabella were buried in the Unitarian chapel in Friargate, Derby.

The Strutt family – Jedediah, his three sons, and their various offspring – were known for their liberal views, support of toleration and humanitarian causes including opposition to slavery.

Their commitment to education embraced Sunday schools and day schools and a number of cultural initiatives far ahead of their time. They insisted on children attending day school before working in the mills (and preferred not to employ children under ten), and attendance at Sunday school for all employees under the age of 20.

They encouraged dancing and provided meeting rooms, and founded a band (actually a 40-piece orchestra) and choir, for whom they provided regular instruction in work time. They organised communal celebrations for events of national importance, and occasionally opened their own gardens for a 'sumptuous déjeuner' of beef, plum pudding, penny loaves and quantities of ale.

The record of their lives, however, is not without ambiguity. They opposed some government reforms, such as the Manufactories Act of 1829, which made it easier to prosecute mill owners. Also, their opposition to slavery has to be qualified by the recognition that the nature of the cotton industry and its global purchasing meant that they continued to buy cotton from slave-owning plantations. This had the effect of perpetuating slavery, despite their campaigning to end the trade in human lives.

Their good reputation as employers who took care of their workforce was inspired by their understanding that all people are part of God's creation, and it was their duty to share the beneficence which God had given them for the benefit of their communities.

A Prayer for Pilgrims

God of innovation and scientific enquiry,

    we give you thanks for Jedediah, William,

    George Benson and Joseph Strutt,

    for their development of industry in Derby and

    the Derwent Valley,

    and for their benevolence to their towns and to their workforce.

May we follow in the way of Christ,

    seeking justice in the complexity of life,

    and working to improve the lives of those in our care.

We pray for all who work in industry today,

    that their work may bring benefit to communities,

    and their profits be used for the good of all.

We ask this in the name of Jesus,

    who spent himself to bring new life to the world.

    Amen.

Derby Arboretum, with some of the architectural elements.

Where to go

Derby:

Jedediah:

A portrait of Jedediah Strutt by Joseph Wright hangs in Derby Art Gallery, and a statue stands on the façade of the building on the corner of East Street and St Peter's Street, DE1 2BL.

His final home at 65 Friar Gate, DE1 1DF was designed by his son William and is marked with a blue plaque. A visit to Pickford's House Museum at No. 41 will give an idea of what it was like inside.

William:

William lived at St Helen's House in King Street, which is marked with a plaque shared with Revd Thomas Gisbourne (Chapter 12). There is a marble bust of him in Derby Museum and Art Gallery.

Joseph:

There is a statue of Joseph in the grand entrance to Derby Arboretum, in Arboretum Square, DE23 8FN. The Arboretum is a Grade II* landscape, gifted to the people of Derby and managed by Derby City Council. Joseph Strutt commissioned the respected botanist and landscape designer John Claudius Loudon to design the park, and Loudon cleverly incorporated landscaped walkways and architectural features which disguise the comparatively small extent of the site. It contains some of the finest examples of unusual tree specimens from around the world including the tulip tree, the Turkish hazel, the Caucasian wingnut and the cucumber tree. It is one of a number of British parks that inspired Central Park in New York.

A portrait of Joseph, who was twice mayor, is owned by the Mayoral Gallery of the Council House, but not currently on display. The Museum and Art Gallery also have several items related to Joseph Strutt in various media, but they are not currently on display.

Thorntree House, DE1 2AE on the site of HSBC bank, was the home which Joseph opened to the public as an Art Gallery and Museum. Artefacts included an Egyptian mummy, now in Derby Museum.

Derby Presbyterian congregation was formed in 1660, and met first at the Chapel of St Mary-on-the-Bridge, DE1 3DD. Thence it moved to a building on Irongate, then, designated as Unitarian, to an imposing purpose-built chapel on Friargate, where Joseph was buried. When demolished in 1974, Joseph's remains were reinterred among a group of Strutt graves at the beautiful Belper Cemetery, DE56 2JE which, appropriately, was originally an arboretum strongly influenced by John Claudius Loudon's writings.

Elsewhere:

Belper:

As Belper is well served by road, rail and bus services it is an easy place to visit.

Although many of the Strutts' mill buildings were cleared in the 1960s, the houses, farms and community buildings have survived. The mill complex and the greater part of the associated housing is all to the north of the town centre, with the houses stretching out in rows and terraces up the slopes of the hills to the north and east. By 1801, about one third of the houses in Belper had been built by the Strutts.

They varied in size and quality to suit the different levels of workers' pockets – the best had a garden, individual lavatory and pigsty.

The North Mill houses a Visitors Centre and Museum, at Bridge Foot, DE56 1YD. There is also an extensive archive of documentary material of interest to industrial and social historians.

The Unitarian Chapel and Chapel Cottage at Field Row, DE56 1DG which Jedediah built in 1788, is Grade II* listed, and contains memorials to members of the family including Jedediah, William and George Benson Strutt.

Belper owes much to the Strutt family. George Henry Strutt (grandson of George Benson Strutt) funded the building of Christ Church, very near the North Mill on Bridge Street, DE56 1BA. The church contains a memorial to him. He later paid for the building of the vicarage next door to the church, and also donated a fire engine to the town in 1889. He paid for the paving of the Market Place and a fountain there was given by the townspeople of Belper in his honour – however it has never worked, as it has never been connected to the water supply.

His son George Herbert, for whom there is a blue plaque at his former home, now the Makeney Hall Hotel, DE56 0RS, gave the Grade II* listed River Gardens, DE56 1FE to the town in 1904. They are largely as originally laid out, with boathouse, tea house and bandstand, and an enlarged promenade next to the river. In 1922, he also gave the Belper Memorial Gardens, DE56 1PZ in memory of those who died in the First World War, on condition that the local council would maintain the site as 'pleasure grounds' and 'place there a suitable cenotaph or monument'.

Cromford:

This extensive UNESCO World Heritage site, DE4 3RQ on its elongated position hemmed in by cliffs, comprises a series of linked mills, warehouses and workshops built between 1771 and 1790. It is the location of the World Heritage Site Gateway Visitor's Centre, and a popular heritage destination, giving a complete picture of an early textile factory complex, with a range of exhibits and small retail outlets.

Milford:

There is no visitor centre, but a leaflet is available at: http://www.milford-makeney.org/wp-content/uploads/2012/05/Hopping-Hill-Meadow.pdf.

Milford Bridge, on Derby Road, DE56 0QE is a river bridge built by William Strutt in 1793, and is Grade II listed; the cantilevered parapet was added in 1906.

Hopping Mill Weir in Foundry Lane, DE56 0RU was an older weir altered by the Strutts in 1799-1801 and is Grade II listed.

Moscow Farm, Derby Road, DE56 0QG was built by the Strutt family in 1812-15 to supply the workforce. It is a large, planned complex including stable, cart sheds, cow sheds, hay barns and domestic accommodation, and is Grade II* listed. It one of a number of such farms.

Milford County Junior Mixed and Infant School in Chevin Road, DE56 0QH, built c.1819-23, is Grade II listed. It was a dual-purpose building, with the ground floor probably used for the wagon and carts for the Strutts' adjoining dye works, and the upper floor as a school.

The children would attend for a few hours each day, combined with a few hours working in the adjoining mill. The water tanks for the dyehouse are still under the school yard.

Holy Trinity Church, DE56 0QH was built in 1846-48 on land given by the Strutts and is Grade II listed. Its unusual north-south alignment is due to the constraints of the site.

Findern:

Jedediah lodged with the Woolatt family at Old Hall, a pair of houses behind those at the church end of Common Piece Lane, DE65 6AF, and married Elizabeth in 1755. The early 18th century Unitarian chapel was demolished in 1939.

South Normanton near Alfreton:

At the time of Jedediah's birth, this was a hamlet with a few dwellings clustered round the church on the hilltop. The historic industries of the village were agriculture, stocking spinning and mining. His birthplace, believed to be in Old Post Office Yard, is now demolished.

Other important mill sites along the river:

Darley Abbey's group of mills and cottages, DE22 1DZ are the best preserved and now used for a variety of commercial uses. Darley Abbey to Derby via Darley Park is a one of a number of pleasant river walks (see http://www.derwentvalleymills.org/visit/where-to-visit-in-the-derwent-valley/. It will bring you to **Lombe's Silk Mill**, DE1 3AF which has just reopened as the Museum of Making, celebrating the area's rich history of innovation over 300 years. (https://www.derbymuseums.org/museum-of-making/)

Also interesting

The River Derwent and its bridges:

Described by Daniel Defoe in 1726 as a 'fury of a river' the Derwent could only be forded at a few particular locations, which nevertheless could still be impassable during winter floods. Wooden bridges provided for a more reliable crossing, but were easily damaged by those same floods. The *History of the County of Derby* of 1829 noted that there were a number of bridges, fords and a ferry across the Derwent and chain bridges for mill workers.

Where necessary, bridges were usually replaced by the local town or county authorities and tradespeople reliant on passable routes, maybe by subscription, as happened when William Strutt was active in Derby. On other occasions, when the bridges were on routes of national importance, their design and construction were approved by parliament, after lengthy negotiation.

Several of the county bridges and stone-arched bridges over the Derwent are now listed structures, and in some cases scheduled monuments; some were built by the local industrial families of the Derwent valley, including the Strutts.

Derby General Infirmary:

William worked closely with his friend, chemist Charles Sylvester on his innovative design for the Derby General Infirmary, which opened in 1810. It displayed the whole range of his architectural and engineering genius: systems of heating and ventilation, baths warmed by steam, a wash house with a revolving drum washing machine, a system for drying linen by hot air, water closets which flushed automatically as a person left the room simultaneously letting in fresh air, and a number of catering innovations such as a roaster and steaming apparatus.

The Infirmary was cubical in shape, surmounted by the dome topped by giant statue of Asclepius, the ancient Greek guardian of medicine and healing. A large staircase rose through the centre of the building, surrounded on each of the three floors by small wards and other rooms. The basement contained the baths, cellars and kitchen, and wash-house, whilst the upper storey housed most of the wards (for between four and eight beds each only), operating rooms, convalescent rooms and the fever wing. Significantly, the middle storey, which was fronted by the main public entrance, contained the chapel, board room, and rooms of the medical staff including Matron. This ensured that any visitors who came through the imposing millstone grit Doric column portico, passed the board room and matron's quarters before going anywhere else, which was important because the building became a showplace visited by medical authorities from all over the country and abroad.

The succession of visitors who toured the Infirmary included natural philosophers, engineers, writers, medical men, royalty, politicians, and architects. Among the royalty were the Grand Duke Nicholas, later Tsar Nicholas I of Russia and Prince Leopold of Saxe-Coburg, later King Leopold I of Belgium. Both spread the reputation of the Strutt-Sylvester developments which found their way into public buildings across Europe – and even on ships negotiating the north-west passage! (see more at https://www.ncbi.nlm.nih.gov/pmc/articles/PMC1044459/).

15. A Passage to India:

Thomas Fanshawe Middleton and William Ward

Kedleston and Derby, 18th-19th centuries

In 1769, two men were born within fifteen miles of one another. Both became missionaries to India, being based again within fifteen miles of one another, and died within a year of one another. Yet there is no record of the two men meeting. Perhaps that is for the best, as they were unlikely to have been natural friends.

The first, Thomas Fanshawe Middleton, was an academic and an establishment figure who found those setting out to preach to Indians to be at best an irritant to his attempts to impose order on the church in India. The second, William Ward, was a self-taught political firebrand who became one of those missionaries whom Middleton found so difficult. Between them they leave a lasting link between Derbyshire and India.

Thomas Fanshawe Middleton

Thomas was born on 28th January 1769 and spent his early years at Kedleston. His father was the Rector of All Saints' Church at the time when it still served a parish. The church still stands but the village has gone, to make way for Kedleston Hall.

Thomas attended Christ's Hospital, a boarding school for those from humbler backgrounds. Education became his main passion and he looked set for a career in the church, studying first at Pembroke College in Cambridge, then being ordained in the Church of England by the Bishop of Lincoln in March 1793. Thomas served his curacy at Gainsborough in Lincolnshire, and was appointed to various posts in Lincolnshire, Huntingdon, and eventually London. He married Elizabeth Maddison of Alvington in Lincolnshire in 1797.

Alongside his career in the church, Middleton was also a scholar of Greek. His work on the Greek article (the word 'the') was distinguished, if hardly a page-turner. He scarcely seemed the kind of person who would go on to pioneering work overseas.

However, in 1812, when he was Archdeacon of Huntingdon, Thomas used his first Charge (an annual address that archdeacons give to their clergy and church wardens) to speak of schools and of the work of the Bible Society. Besides being interested in the Bible Society, Thomas also regularly attended meetings of the Society for the Promotion of Christian Knowledge (SPCK). In 1813, the SPCK asked him to deliver another Charge, in this case a special sermon given to those about to be ordained, to a man being ordained priest to serve in southern India. Thomas' support for education and for mission was becoming clear.

In 1814, as part of the renewal of their Charter by Parliament, the East India Company was required to appoint a bishop to serve in India, and to make a diocese (the area governed by a bishop) to cover all of their territory. The enormous area to be encompassed by the new diocese covered the whole of what is now modern India and also what are now Pakistan, Bangladesh and Burma, and even the continent of Australia. The Bishop of Lincoln suggested the name of Thomas Fanshawe Middleton to the President of the Board of Commission for India, and he was asked to be the bishop. Initially tempted to refuse,

Thomas finally agreed to serve. 'I trust in the Almighty to bless the work in which I am to engage', he said.

Thomas' consecration as the first Bishop of Calcutta (known today as Kolkata) was done quietly on the 8th May 1814. The East India Company feared that it could upset the Hindus, Muslims, Sikhs and Buddhists, which would be bad for trade. A month later, Thomas sailed for India.

On the voyage Thomas indulged his academic interests, studying Hebrew and learning Persian. He also wrote some short rules for his life as Bishop of Calcutta. These include preaching frequently; promoting schools, charities, literature, and good taste; never to be in a hurry; to rise early; to advise and encourage youth; and to remember the final judgement. These rules are a mixture of good sense, Victorian manners, and commitment to God.

Thomas landed in Calcutta in November 1814, without being noticed by the authorities. His first sermon was preached on Christmas Day, and he recorded that 'the Churchmen [Anglicans] are abundantly well satisfied, while the Methodists are pleased to find that the Bishop is a Christian. I wish, if possible, to bring them together'. From these quiet and inauspicious beginnings, Thomas went about the job of bringing order to his enormous diocese. He described the task ahead of him as 'a vast extent of seemingly impenetrable jungle'.

His first challenge was to establish systems of governance for the church in India. He appointed archdeacons for Bombay and Madras and conducted lengthy tours of the diocese. These kept him away from home for months at a time and took him all over India. During these trips, he met people from a range of different cultures, languages and religions. Throughout, he built mission stations and encouraged the teaching of the faith to any who wanted to learn. Slightly perplexed by German missionaries sent by the Church Mission Society, he remarked that 'I must either license them or silence them', and so he embraced those of different traditions within the church. Schools were also part of his work, and he established many and reformed those already there. Under his care, the church grew and was respected across the sub-continent.

Thomas Middleton's appointment was initially intended to be about the support of British Christians living and working in India. As he grew in knowledge of his diocese, and in confidence in his position, Thomas wanted to involve the people of India more. There were large and growing Indian congregations of Christians, and Middleton discovered the story that one of Jesus' twelve disciples (Thomas), had brought Christianity to India in the first century. But he was forbidden, by the terms of his appointment and by law, to ordain native Indians to serve the church. So Thomas Middleton took the long view. He raised funds from England to build a college, the aims of which were to instruct the young (both expatriate and native) in Christianity so that they could preach and teach; teach English; translate the Bible; and be a place where English missionaries could come and learn about the country where they had come to work.

Bishop's College in Calcutta opened in 1820, and Thomas recruited a noted scholar to be the first principal. However, it would take about a century for the College to begin to train Indians for ordination, and finally to accomplish all of its purposes – and Thomas' intentions.

As well as his organisational work, Thomas kept his rule to preach regularly. This was the foundation of his ministry. He also wrote a hymn, which was sung on New Year's Day. The first line of the hymn is 'As o'er the past my memory strays' and it bemoans the lack of preparation to meet God after death. It is, however, a hopeful hymn, and asks God to chase despair away, 'Thy grace it is which prompts the prayer, that grace can do the rest'.

Illness was a regular element of his time in India, beginning six months into his ministry in Calcutta, and in the evening of 8th July 1822, aged only 53, Thomas died of sunstroke. He was buried under the altar of St John's Church in Calcutta, the Cathedral at that time. After his death, news reached India that he had been made a governor of his old school, Christ's Hospital. Whilst Thomas never knew of his appointment, the link was enough for his widow to send the child of her widowed Indian friend to study in England. Thomas would have been very pleased that his old school was educating a child from India, where he had worked to bring education and faith to all.

William Ward

William Ward was born in Derby on 20th October 1769, the son of a carpenter. His father, John, died when William was young, and so he was brought up by his mother. She took him to the local Wesleyan Methodist Chapel. Without much formal education, William became apprenticed to a printer in Derby, Mr Drewry, and on completing his apprenticeship, aged 19, he became the editor of the weekly *Derby Mercury*. He used this paper to champion social improvement projects and campaign against the slave trade. Thomas Clarkson, one of the leaders of that campaign, came to visit William in Derby, and following Clarkson's visit, William ran more stories, and included more gruesome detail about the treatment of slaves. Despite complaints from some subscribers, he continued as editor for six years, publishing nearly 100,000 words on the horrors of the slave trade.

William Ward was also involved in the Derby Society for Political Information, a radical group. He composed political manifestos, which led to him being prosecuted for seditious libel. He went to London for his trial, and then again to study print-typography. It was during this time, on 31st March 1793, that he met William Carey, a Baptist missionary preparing to go to India. Carey told him, 'I hope, by God's blessing, to have the Bible translated and ready for press in four or five years. You must come and print it for us'.

From London, William moved to Hull, again to edit a newspaper, and he was baptised in a Particular Baptist Church. He only lasted nine months as an editor in Hull, before returning to Derby and getting involved in more political controversy. Fearing imprisonment, he went back to Hull, and spent his time studying the Bible. In 1797, he began to study to become a Baptist minister at Ewood Hall in Halifax, and offered himself as a missionary to India. In a service on 1st May 1799, he was set apart for the work of a Christian missionary and by October he had landed in Calcutta to join William Carey.

On board the *Criterion*, the ship that took him to India, William began a journal which continues to be read as a history of the mission work. Equally significantly, he met Joshua Marshman, also being sent out to be a missionary. Controversy continued to follow William, and instead of presenting himself innocuously as an assistant in Carey's indigo business, he announced their much more disruptive missionary purpose. Consequently, the two had to flee twelve miles upriver to the Danish colony of Serampore, where British law did not run, as the East India Company was very hostile to their presence. Carey himself gave up the indigo plant and the financial security it provided, and joined William Ward and Joshua Marshman in Serampore. They were to become known as the "Serampore Trio'.

The trio of Carey, Marshman and Ward proved to be highly effective. William Carey was a translator and the best known of the three. He travelled around overseeing missionary work. Joshua Marshman was an educationalist and set about making the Serampore mission self-financing. His determination and zeal at times brought him into conflict with Carey. William Ward, the firebrand back at home, became the peacemaker, and it was he who was chosen to be the pastor to the new church at Serampore. He was a gifted preacher, especially in Bengali, and a famous engraving shows him baptising a Hindu convert in the River Ganges.

In Serampore, William Ward married Mary Tidd Fountain, the widow of another missionary. She had a son from her first marriage, and together they had several daughters. Ward also became an 'uncle' to many younger members of the Serampore mission, befriending and mentoring them.

William Ward's skills as a printer were very important to the mission. Over thirty years, Serampore produced six translations of the whole Bible, twenty-three translations of the New Testament, and portions of the Bible in a further ten languages – a prodigious output. William printed them all, engaging type cutters and casters to create the fonts of typefaces for some 20 Indian languages, many for the first time, at least one with 700 characters. In 1812, a fire destroyed the printing office and the type for all the scriptures that had been printed. Fortunately, the moulds for the metal castings were recovered, and from these William managed to reconstruct the type. He himself wrote a book, *Account of the Writings, Religion, and Manners of the Hindoos* which he published in 1806. It was a careful and widely read account of Indian culture.

In 1818, Ward returned to England, partly to aid his recovery from illness, but also to raise funds for a college that the Serampore Trio had founded. The college opened in 1819, with 37 students, in equal numbers of Christians and non-Christians. Their aim was to educate Indians, and especially native preachers. The college, now a university, was given its charter by the King of Denmark in 1827.

Only eighteen months after his return to Serampore, William Ward died. On 5th March 1823 he had preached and seemed in excellent health, yet two days later, 7th March, he had been taken by cholera and was dead. He was buried in the mission at Serampore. At his funeral service, Joshua Marshman spoke of him as a 'pastor to the pastors of India'.

There is much that divided Thomas Fanshawe Middleton and William Ward in life. Yet there are tantalising points of convergence, both in the colleges they both worked so hard to found, and in the way that each worked to support the work of others. Neither brought skills that immediately seem to speak of bringing good news to a different culture, but in the organisational skills they each had, both were effective.

The desire that Middleton expressed after his first Christmas in India, to bring together the Anglicans and the Methodists, has now been accomplished. United churches, the Church of North India and the Church of South India, have been formed from those two denominations along with the Congregationalists and Presbyterians. The Church of North India is linked with the churches of Derbyshire, and it is tempting to suggest that the lives of both Thomas Fanshawe Middleton and William Ward have played a part in this. Visits in both directions are a regular part of church life in Derbyshire, and this has recently extended to schools. That, too, would have pleased both men.

It is sometimes said that if you want to make God laugh, just tell him your plans. The lives of Thomas Fanshawe Middleton and William Ward show the surprising changes that can happen in life. Middleton's diligence in creating systems, in planning for the long term, and his deep care for education were things that God used to build the church and to enable others to flourish. Ward's background in radical politics enabled him to be a peacemaker and pastor, and his printing skills were the bedrock of a major centre of Bible translation. The establishment scholar of obscure and technical elements of language and the fire-brand printer with no formal education are both saints who brought good news to many.

A Prayer for Pilgrims

God of organisation and of passion,

    we give you thanks for Thomas Fanshawe Middleton

    and William Ward,

    for their response to your surprising call,

    for their care for education for all people,

    and for their desire to bring Christians together.

May we follow in the way of Christ,

    showing courage to do unexpected things,

    hope in planning for the long term,

    and love for those who are different from us.

We pray for all who share the Good News in different cultures,

    that they may recognise your call in different people,

    and share your love across divides.

We ask this in the name of Jesus,

    whose grace prompts our prayer and does all that we need.

    Amen.

The illustration brings together motifs from around the south door of Kedleston church, books which William Ward printed, and a section of the ivory overlay of a mahogany chest in Kedleston Hall's Oriental Room.

Where to go

Neither Middleton nor Ward have memorials in Derbyshire to the best of our knowledge.

Kedleston:

The parish church at Kedleston has memorials to the Curzon family, and not least to the Lord Curzon who was Viceroy of India, and Lady Mary his wife, the Vicereine. Kedleston Hall makes a great deal of Curzon's time as Viceroy. (see 'Also interesting', following)

However, there is no memorial in either the church or the Hall to the earlier connection between Kedleston and India in Thomas Fanshawe Middleton. Kedleston Church is, however, where Thomas was baptised and spent his early years.

Derby:

The printer's shop where Ward was apprenticed was until recently Lloyds Bank at the corner of Irongate and Sadlergate in Derby. However, its links with Ward and Serampore are not acknowledged.

Elsewhere:

If you are in London, you can find the memorial sculpture of Thomas Fanshawe Middleton in the second bay of the south aisle of St Paul's Cathedral.

And in Kolkata, his burial place is marked by a memorial slab in front of the altar of St. John's Church, and an interesting account of his funeral is included in
https://indianvagabond.com/2019/05/13/thomas-fanshawe-middleton-last-resting-place/

Also interesting

More about All Saints Church, Kedleston:

Essentially thirteenth century, All Saints' church is all that remains of the medieval village of Kedleston, razed in 1759 by Sir Nathaniel Curzon to make way for the magnificent Kedleston Hall. The Curzon family has lived at Kedleston for 700 years and their stunning memorials - created by several famous designers including Robert Adam - fill the church.

The grandest of these, in white alabaster floating on a sea of green translucent quartz, was erected in 1909 in a specially built side chapel, for Lord Curzon's wife, the Vicereine Mary. In her time in Imperial India, Mary was responsible for a number of important medical reforms for the care of women. She also helped revive traditional Indian crafts by influencing master craftspeople to adapt their designs to European tastes and by facilitating trade. Indian materials and motifs thus became highly fashionable in European cities. It has recently been speculated that she and her daughters inspired the main characters of popular TV series 'Downton Abbey'.

The church's oldest feature is the Norman south doorway, which has zigzag moulding and grotesque bird heads. Look out for the carving of the fiendish little faces of horseman and wild beasts that glare out at you just above the door!

Derby church links with the Church in North India:

Throughout Derbyshire, many churches have links with the Church in North India. St Peter's-in-the-City in Derby, DE1 1SN hosts an annual

'Christmas Lunch on Jesus', which feeds families at Christmas in both Derby and Kolkata (see www.stpetersderby.org.uk).

The illustration of William Ward:

The print of "William Ward baptizing a Hindoo in the Ganges at Serampore", (1821) from a painting by John Jackson, is held by the British Museum and can be found at https://en.wikipedia.org/wiki/William_Ward_(missionary).

William Ward's publications:

A view of the history, literature, and mythology of the Hindoos by William Ward.

This 1822 edition was arranged according to the order of the original work printed at Serampore and is held in the Special Collections of the British Library (BL1201.W2)

The East India Company:

The East India Company was one of the most powerful and enduring organisations in history and had a long lasting impact on the Indian Subcontinent.

It received its original royal charter from Queen Elizabeth I in 1600, and by the early 19th Century the Company controlled most of the subcontinent. It was at the heart of British imperial policy, with Queen Victoria becoming Empress of India in 1876. The British Crown took over direct rule (The Raj) from 1858 to 1947.

16. Nursing and Numbers:

Florence Nightingale

Lea, 19th–20th centuries

Named for the city in which she was born and baptised, Florence Nightingale achieved worldwide recognition during her own lifetime, and that fame has continued to grow since her death. She is by far the most well known of all Derbyshire saints, remembered all over the world for her work to develop the nursing profession – there is even a portrait of her hanging on the wall of matron's office in the hospital at Serenga in north India.

Florence was born on 12th May 1820, into a family rooted in the campaign against the slave trade, quite wealthy, and with a variety of religious affiliations. She was baptised on 4th July 1820 by an Anglican priest, Dr Thomas Trevor, a Prebendary of Chester, and she maintained her Anglican faith throughout her life.

The Nightingale family had an estate at Lea in Derbyshire. Florence moved there when she was just a year old, but did not take to the climate.

A cough and persistent sore throat marked her childhood. She also had to wear steel lined boots until she was in her late teens, to correct her feet. But Lea was a place where Florence was happy and began to explore the path on which she would continue for all her life. Nevertheless, she spent much of her youth suffering from bouts of depression and feeling stifled by the lethargy and helplessness of women of her class, rejecting their life of thoughtless comfort.

The family home, Lea Hurst

She was taught at home by her father, receiving an excellent education in maths and science as well as classical and modern languages. From an early age she accompanied her mother in visiting those who were sick and poor in the locality. By her late teens, Florence was making such visits herself and was often missing for the evening meal because she was sitting with someone who was ill. Her sister wrote to their grandmother in 1836 that 'Flo has been very busy paying visits to the village. The people about here are very fond of her, & she likes them & is always sorry to leave them'.

On 7th February 1837, Florence was staying at the family's other house in Hampshire when 'God spoke to me and called me to his service'. This sense of call was something that would be repeated over the coming years as Florence tried to discern what it meant. Clearly it was something which would be foundational to Florence's future career, and trying to tease out the meaning was a subject to which she returned frequently. Ultimately, and after many painful disagreements within her family, it would lead to Florence turning away from the expected role of wife and mother. Instead, she would serve God through serving others.

Florence then began a long search for what form that service would take, but by 1850, she had become convinced that nursing was at the core of her call to service. Her family were initially horrified because this was regarded as rather degrading work of a sort usually carried out for example by the camp followers of the army, and thus associated with women of low repute.

Florence took a place at the Protestant Institute for Deaconesses in Kaiserswerth near Dusseldorf. Here she received a somewhat inadequate medical training, alongside hearing frequent sermons and attending Bible classes taught by Pastor Flieder and other Lutheran ministers. Above all, she was among other women who shared her sense of calling. Her conviction that women could be called and used in the service of God was deepened. Coming back to Britain, she overcame resistance from her family and took a post as matron at the Institute for Gentlewomen in Upper Harley Street in London in 1853.

After also volunteering at a cholera outbreak in a Middlesex hospital, Florence realised just how bad sanitary practices were in English hospitals, and decided it would be her life's work to improve them. She lived at a time when causes of disease were not well understood, but she held strong views about the importance of clean air, calm environments and kindness in health and healing, in contrast to the more mechanistic view prevailing in the medical profession.

Florence's fame came from her contribution to the nursing of soldiers during the Crimean War. When reports came back about the terrible conditions for those wounded, Florence gathered a staff of women volunteer nurses. Her political skills, fierce determination, and social connections came together as she lobbied Sidney Herbert, the Secretary for War and a close friend, to allow them to travel to the Crimea to help.

In November 1854, Florence and her team were assigned to a military hospital at Selimiye Barracks in Scutari. There they found that conditions were at least as bad as the reports had suggested. It was horrifically understaffed and literally sat on top of a cesspool which contaminated the entire building. When they reached the hospital, the group found thousands of patients crammed into tiny, filthy cells, dying in their own excrement. Even the most basic necessities like soap and bandages were in short supply. Ten times more soldiers were dying from illnesses such as typhus, cholera and dysentery than from wounds received in battles. Many were starving from lack of proper food, as there were no cooking facilities. The hospital's death rate had soared to over 42 percent.

After scrubbing down the hospital and removing a dead horse that was contaminating the drinking water supply, Florence created an organised kitchen and put a chef in charge. Finally, the patients were getting the food they needed so that their bodies could heal. She also established a laundry, classroom, and library, and made sure the patients had intellectual stimulation and entertainment. She made sure her nurses washed their hands regularly – a practice that was not implemented in the medical profession until she came along!

Amidst endless opposition to her work and despite an extreme lack of supplies, Florence managed to reduce the hospital's death rate from 42% to just 2% during the Crimean War. Concurrently, she lobbied government, wrote to the newspapers and collected evidence.

The changes that Florence introduced and urged dramatically reduced the death rates. But it was her care for those who were sick, often sitting with them late into the night, that won her the affectionate name of 'the Lady with the Lamp'. The time spent as a teenager sitting at the bedsides of the ill of Derbyshire gave her the skills to nurse the injured of Scutari.

The lamp used by Florence Nightingale in Scutari, now in the Florence Nightingale Museum, London

Her experience in Crimea had a profound effect on the rest of her career. She thoroughly believed that the death rates were entirely due to poor nutrition, appalling sanitation, lack of supplies, stale air, and lack of proper rest. Those beliefs would spur her to entirely reshape the nursing profession for all time, a campaign that she developed through the rest of her life.

The Crimean conflict was resolved in 1856, and Florence returned to her childhood home. Entirely to her surprise, she was met with a hero's welcome. She met Queen Victoria and obtained her support for a Royal Commission on the health of the army, through which she was instrumental in improving soldiers' living conditions.

With a testimonial fund of £50,000, Florence founded training schools for nurses (the first being at St Thomas' Hospital in London) and wrote *Notes on Nursing: What it is and What it is not* (1859) which became the standard textbook not only for her own school but around the world. In harmony with new thinking amongst doctors and engineers, she propelled a real change in attitudes towards healthful buildings for the care of the sick, which resulted in the wide adoption of the 'Nightingale plan' ward as the standard.

Florence was an impressive and versatile writer and campaigner – later in life she wrote over 200 books and pamphlets covering medical knowledge, religion and mysticism, including an essay considered to be an early feminist work. She exploited her newfound fame ruthlessly, campaigning successfully for social reforms including the introduction of trained nurses into workhouses, and opposing the regulation of prostitution as a means of controlling contagious disease.

Less well known is that Florence believed in a statistical approach to viewing problems. She was one of the first statisticians to use diagrams to convey statistical information. We would call these infographics today, and they make understanding the information much easier. Florence's most famous infographic is a polar area graph which shows mortality in the British army (see https://en.wikipedia.org/wiki/Florence_Nightingale#/media/File:Nightingale-mortality.jpg).

For Florence, statistics were important because they helped in finding the root causes of problems and thus enabled prevention, not just the treatment of symptoms. Florence saw statistics as a way of listening to God's voice. 'To understand God's thoughts one must study statistics', she wrote, because they are 'the measure of his purpose'. Florence saw God as a co-worker with human beings. This was rooted in her reading of the Bible. She regarded the book of Leviticus as being about preventing evil, more than removing it. This led to her attempts to prevent disease, crime and poverty rather than fixing the problems after they had arisen. She once described the Bengal Sanitary Commissioners as 'God's great missionaries in India'. Florence's faith was very practical, and she had little patience for sentimental or romantic faith that could not address reality. Even her understanding of prayer was influenced by her statistical approach: 'it is against God's will to pray that the typhus caused by the foul drain should be removed without the drain being removed'.

Florence's faith was clearly at the root of her care and social action. Her call, which she often referred to as her 'business', ran deeply within her. Throughout her life she read the Bible, theology and devotional books. She annotated her Bible extensively, showing her continuing interest and engagement with it. Yet she rarely attended church. She received communion at home from Benjamin Jowett, a priest and professor at Oxford. Her influence on this scholar priest was such that it was Florence who introduced him to the Christian mystics, and she wrote sermons for him that he later preached.

Florence saw God as a generous father who forgives, corrects and guides his children. Religion could be hard work: essentially, it was cooperation with God, through studying God's laws to see how and where to intervene in order to solve problems. Prayer, she wrote, requires 'the highest exercise of the intellect as well as the deepest affect of the heart'. And Florence saw clearly that women were also called to this cooperation with God. She understood the way that Jesus gave women a higher place than the society of this time did. She argued with those who would prevent women from preaching. And she regularly used feminine language for God. 'Father to me thou art and mother too and sister dear'.

As she grew older, Florence became physically weaker. While in the Crimea she had fallen ill with 'Crimean Fever' or typhus, which affected her for the rest of her life, so she was often confined to her room. Yet she continued to see people and to write. She was writing papers well into her seventies, until blindness and failing mental faculties began to prevent her.

She was awarded the Order of Merit in the UK in 1907 and also honoured by the German, French and Norwegian governments for her work.

Florence died aged 90, in her sleep, on 13th August 1910. She was buried in the family church in Hampshire, having declined the offer to be buried in Westminster Abbey.

Florence Nightingale was a saint who had a deep call and a clear vision of what God asked of her. She wanted to cooperate with God, and this led to her particular combination of compassion with hard-headed analysis. Florence shows us how to hold together the head and the heart, and the powerful combination which that can be in the service of God's call.

'If I could give you information of my life, it would be to show how a woman of very ordinary ability has been led by God in strange and unaccustomed paths to do in His service what He has done in her. And if I could tell you all, you would see how God has done all, and I nothing'.

A Prayer for Pilgrims

God of compassion and of purpose,

> we give you thanks for Florence Nightingale,

> for her care for the sick and those in need,

> for her clear analysis of what caused their state,

> and for her relentless work to improve their lives.

May we follow in the way of Christ,

> holding care and clear thinking together,

> and being determined to change this world.

We pray for nurses and all who care for the sick,

> that they may show your care for the suffering,

> and know your call for justice.

We ask this in the name of Jesus,

> who tells us that to care for others is to care for him.

> Amen.

Head, hands and heart: including the polar area graph and the lamp shown in some of the statues of Florence Nightingale.

Where to go

Lea:

The Nightingales' house in Lea is still there, at DE4 5AT, with a blue plaque on the gateway – though it is currently a private home.

It was originally a 17th century farmhouse which Florence's father William inherited from his great-uncle Peter Nightingale, in 1815. Elizabeth Gaskell stayed here in October 1854 and left a charming description of the place:

'High as Lea Hurst is, one seems on a pinnacle, with the clouds careering around one. Down below is a garden with stone terraces and flights of steps – the planes of these terraces being perfectly gorgeous with masses of hollyhocks, dahlias, nasturtiums, geraniums etc. Then a sloping meadow losing itself in a steep wooded descent (such tints over the wood!) to the River Derwent, the rocks on the other side of which form the first distance, and are of a red colour streaked with misty purple. Beyond this, interlacing hills, forming three ranges of distance; the first, deep brown with decaying heather; the next, in some purple shadow, and the last catching some pale, watery sunlight'.

It is easy to imagine Florence communing with the divine and contemplating what her future might hold.

Derby:

There is a magnificent statue of Florence on London Road, DE1 2QY, and her influence is evident in some of the street names nearby. Where Derby's main hospital once stood there is a new estate known as the Nightingale Quarter, which is fitting because she had some input into the design of the previous hospital building. In 1860, Dr William Ogle was appointed to the Derbyshire General Infirmary at a time when the mortality rate amongst patients was high. After much lengthy correspondence with Florence, it was decided to have a complete rebuild of the hospital along lines suggested by her. Designed by H.I. Stevens, the new Derby Royal Infirmary opened in 1894 with a new wing named after her, a chapel, operating theatres, kitchen, laundry and mortuary.

The Florence Nightingale window, which was installed in the hospital chapel in 1960, is now in the church of St Peter-in-the-city, DE1 1NN. Across the road from St Peter's, a small statue of Florence can be seen on the façade of the building at the junction with East St, DE1 2BL, and there is another above the Nightingale-Macmillan Continuing Care Unit opposite the newer Royal Derby Hospital, DE22 3NE. A memorial plaque to Florence can also be seen in Derby Cathedral, DE1 3GP.

Florence also has a star in the 'Made in Derby Walk of Fame' running from Albion Street, DE1 2PR to Exchange Street, DE1 2DU. Download the app, point it at the star and a virtual reality Florence Nightingale will appear. More details at https://www.visitderby.co.uk/whats-on/made-in-derby-ii/.

Also interesting

Dethick Chapel:

The bells of quiet and secluded Dethick Chapel, DE4 5GG welcomed Florence Nightingale from the Crimea to neighbouring Lea. NB: The church is up a track through Church Farm, with access on foot only.

The Florence Nightingale Medal:

Awarded by the International Committee of Red Cross (ICRC) the Florence Nightingale Medal is the highest international distinction within the nursing profession. It is awarded to people who distinguish themselves in times of peace or war by showing exceptional courage and devotion to the wounded, sick or disabled or to civilian victims of conflict or disaster.

Bank notes:

Florence Nightingale's image appeared on the reverse of £10 Series D banknotes issued by the Bank of England from 1975 until 1994. As well as a standing portrait, she was depicted on the notes in a field hospital, holding her lamp, and prior to 2002, other than the female monarchs, she was the only woman whose image had ever adorned British paper currency.

Florence Nightingale Museum:

This is located at parking level in the grounds of St Thomas' Hospital, London, SE1 7EW, a short walk from the Houses of Parliament and the London Eye.

17. Ashbourne and the Army:

Catherine Booth

Ashbourne, 19th century

The 'Mother of the Salvation Army', Catherine Booth, was born in Ashbourne on 17th January 1829. Catherine had four brothers, but only one lived to adulthood. Her parents John and Sarah Mumford were members of a Wesleyan chapel, and John had been a local preacher. At some point during Catherine's childhood, however, he lost his faith, though her mother remained a zealous Methodist and this had a major impact on Catherine as she grew up. Sarah prevented Catherine from playing with other children in case she caught bad habits. She also forbade her from reading novels, which she saw as the work of the devil. Above all, Sarah was anxious that Catherine should not learn French.

As well as the restrictions of her mother's fierce religiosity, Catherine's childhood was marked by illness. Suffering from spinal curvature, she spent long periods of time lying flat on her back. There was little to do but to read. Catherine's lifelong love of the Bible and theology can be dated to this time in her adolescence. One famous story about her is that she had read the Bible through entirely eight times before her twelfth birthday. Her mother's prohibition of novels was relaxed a little for Catherine to read John Bunyan's *Pilgrim's Progress*. Catherine enjoyed it but was critical of its Calvinist theology. She consistently rejected any notion of 'the elect' throughout her life and ministry.

The Mumford family moved away from Ashbourne, first to Boston in Lincolnshire which was John Mumford's home town. He and Catherine were active in the Boston temperance movement and wrote articles for a temperance magazine. Temperance, the movement against drinking alcohol, had been an important feature of Methodism from the beginning. It can be seen as a reaction to the way in which drink made other social problems, such as poverty, unemployment and domestic violence, much worse. This was the first of Catherine's many campaigns for social improvement, which were a constituent part of her faith. She once chased a collier down the street and tried to grab the hammer from his hand, after she saw him hit his donkey with it. She also anticipated later campaigns by giving up sugar as a protest against the treatment of black slaves.

By the time the family moved south to Brixton in London, Catherine was a very gifted theologian. It was there, at the age of sixteen, that she experienced a revelation that convinced her that she was saved. On 15th June 1846, she was reading a hymn by Charles Wesley and wrote that, 'I no longer hoped that I was saved. I was certain of it'. Her theological convictions became firmer, and in 1850 she was expelled by the Wesleyan Methodists and joined the Methodist Reformers, for whom she ran a girls' Sunday school in Clapham.

The following year, at a tea party at the home of factory owner Edward Rabbits, she met William Booth. William had also been expelled from the Wesleyan Methodists, but Edward Rabbits, who was an enthusiastic Methodist Reformer, recognised his preaching gift and had been supporting the penniless William financially.

The first encounter between Catherine and William did not go well. William admitted that he was not a total abstainer from alcohol, and Catherine attacked him on the issue. William later spoke of falling in love with Catherine at first sight – clearly, he had forgotten their first meeting and was thinking of a later tea party. This one was on Good Friday 1852, the very day when William began life as a full-time preacher. So began a partnership, formed in love and prayer, that would transform many lives. Catherine and William were both stern, moralistic and courageous. They shared a deep and lively faith, and sought to share that faith with others.

During their engagement, which was to last three years, Catherine and William formed a formidable partnership. Catherine brought an intellectual depth that William never had himself but which he valued highly. With her encouragement and strategic mind, William became a Congregationalist minister, before returning to the Methodist fold. Neither Catherine nor William were wedded to any particular denomination, although they did have strong theological opinions. This 'church juggling' enabled William to have a base, and crucially an income, that would allow him to cement his ministry as a preacher, and eventually allow the couple to be married. William's career found a firmer footing as an itinerant evangelist travelling all over the country preaching. Finally, on 17th June 1855, Catherine Mumford married William Booth in a Congregational church in Stockwell Green. Characteristically it was a simple wedding, leaving all available money and energy for ministry. Their honeymoon on the Isle of Wight included preaching engagements for William, who left for Yorkshire as soon as they returned to London.

Prior to their marriage, the couple had perhaps their only major argument. It led to a sixteen-page letter from Catherine to William which contained an ultimatum – William was to agree with her or the wedding was off. What was at stake was the equality of women within Christianity. For Catherine, this was at the heart of what made her a Christian. 'Oh, what endears the Christian religion to my heart is what it *has* done and *is destined* to do for my own sex'. Indeed, since she had been a girl, this had been a non-negotiable condition of marrying any man. Catherine had read the Bible carefully and was able to reject the standard interpretation that forbade women to preach and lead worship in church. Instead, she pointed to St Paul's declaration that 'in Christ there is ... no male and female' (Galatians 3.28) and the fulfilment of the prophecy that 'your daughters shall prophesy' in the Acts of the Apostles (Acts 2). When an American evangelist, Phoebe Palmer, toured England in 1859, the final piece fell into place for Catherine: she now had experience of a woman actually doing what she had long argued for. By now she also had William's support, and wrote a pamphlet *Female Ministry: Women's Right to Preach* (1859) which set out her arguments. From there it was natural that she would begin to preach herself. In January 1860, she preached for the first time at one of William's gatherings in Gateshead.

That began Catherine's own ministry as a preacher and evangelist. At first, hand-bills advertised her meetings under the heading 'Come and hear a woman preach', making the most of the novelty. But as her preaching ministry grew, and at least one bishop urged his (male) clergy to attend to her as an example of how to preach with power and effect. Nevertheless, it was Catherine who raised the eight children that were born to the couple.

After a long period of travelling around the country, sometimes together and sometimes apart, Catherine and William settled in London in 1865. William became the minister of the East London Mission. At first it seemed that this would simply be a short respite from the demands of travelling. But as Catherine and William began to work, they began to change their vision. They started to encounter those on the very edge of society: alcoholics, prostitutes, and addicts. William preached to them and found that many turned to the Gospel message. Meanwhile Catherine, continuing to share in the ministry, spoke to groups of wealthier people. She became the bread winner for the family and for the Mission. In May 1878, William was dictating a letter and described the Mission as 'a volunteer army'. After his son remonstrated that he was no volunteer, William changed the phrase to 'salvation army'. The name stuck and became the whole means of organising the operation. The Army had a flag, with the phrase 'Blood and Fire' emblazoned on it. Ministry was undertaken by Officers, who all wore uniforms. William took the rank of General. Catherine took no rank. She became known as the 'Mother of the Salvation Army'. But she did ensure that from the very start, women served as officers alongside men. The right of women to preach was written into the foundation deed of the Salvation Army.

With its origins in the most deprived parts of London, the Salvation Army has always worked hard at caring for the poorest and most vulnerable members of society. The Army's rallying cry became 'soup, soap and salvation'. Catherine was dedicated to this work and identified with the daily struggles of the poor. She worked to secure better conditions and pay for women workers in the matchstick-making industry. Her involvement with prostitutes led her to a clear-sighted vision of the need to combine evangelism and social action. She challenged comfortable Christians to take their responsibility for the conditions in which people worked. She would even preach to royalty and did not hesitate to approach Queen Victoria to change oppressive laws. It was Catherine who persuaded William, and the wider Salvation Army, that prostitution was not an issue about women, but one about men. This is a perspective that still has much to contribute to debates about social policy today.

In 1880, the Salvation Army started work in Australia, Ireland and the United States. From there it has grown, so that today it is at work in 131 countries. It consistently provides for the poorest, the homeless and the victims of disasters. It continues to gather for worship, for preaching and for evangelism. Women are still seen as equal participants in its leadership and ministry. It has become a world-renowned and respected organisation because of its care for the poorest, and works with the strapline of 'Transforming lives in every community'.

Much of this is due to Catherine. The partnership that she forged with William provided energy, strategy and intellect. Her care for the poorest, and her fierce belief in the equality of women and men, have had a long-lasting legacy. Both came out of her deep, biblical and evangelical faith. Throughout her life she struggled with illness and was frequently confined to bed, but she never gave up, and constantly worked to preach the Gospel to anyone who would listen.

A collection of Catherine's sermons is entitled *Aggressive Christianity* (1883). That is a good summary of Catherine Booth's faith and life. She died, or (as Salvationists would say, 'was promoted to glory') in

October 1890, aged 61, and more than 36,000 mourners attended her funeral. Her last sermon spoke of what regrets would be faced in the light of eternity: 'that we have done so much? Oh, no! That we have done so little'.

Catherine Booth is a saint who demonstrates both concern for the poor, and concern for the reasons that people are trapped in poverty. She speaks of the equality of women and men, and of the power of God to change lives. Even in the midst of debilitating illness, she found she was able to serve others. She was uncompromising in her preaching and in her life. Through her, many others have been helped and have found new life in the Christian faith.

A Prayer for Pilgrims

God of the poorest,

>we give you thanks for Catherine Booth,

>for her conviction of the truth of the Gospel,

>for her life among the poor and vulnerable,

>and for her vision of the equality of women and men.

May we follow in the way of Christ,

>working to bring justice for those who suffer,

>treating all people as worthy of respect and opportunity,

>and holding tenaciously to what is true.

We pray for all who live in poverty,

>that they may find your provision for their need

>and be given the dignity of the children of God.

We ask this in the name of Jesus,

>who preached good news to the poor.

>Amen.

'Praise Him with timbrel and dance' (Ps 150:4)

Where to Go

Ashbourne:

There is a bust of Catherine in Ashbourne Park, DE6 1EJ, the town of her birth, and a simple plaque above the door of her birthplace at 13 Sturston Lane, DE6 1BA – although it is now Sturston Road, rather than Sturston Lane. The chapel that she attended has now been replaced by a new chapel in Church Street, DE6 2AQ.

Elsewhere in Derbyshire:

The Salvation Army is very active in Derbyshire, and can be found in Alfreton, Buxton, Chesterfield, Clay Cross, Derby, Ripley and Somercotes.

London:

The chief memorials to Catherine and William are in London: twin statues outside the Salvation Army's William Booth Memorial Training College, on Champion Park, Camberwell, SE5 8BQ, and replicas near Trinity Green Almshouses in Mile End Road, E1 4TS, where they began their ministry.

18. Stronger Together:

Herbert Henry Elvin and Olave Baden-Powell

Eckington and Chesterfield, 19ᵗʰ and 20ᵗʰ centuries

Coming from different ends of the social spectrum, Herbert Henry Elvin and Olave Baden-Powell brought their faith, energy and gifts to building up movements that would benefit others.

Herbert Henry Elvin

Herbert Henry Elvin was born on 18ᵗʰ July 1874, in Eckington at the northern-most edge of Derbyshire. A committed Baptist, he left school at 14 and became a preacher the following year. After spending time in India, he returned to England to study at the People's Palace (the precursor to Queen Mary College in London, which maintains links with India). From there he went on to study at Birkbeck College and the City of London College.

Once in employment in 1894, Herbert joined the National Union of Clerks and Administration Workers. This was to become his great vocation. He engaged in more and more union work, holding a variety of posts, culminating in becoming the Honorary Secretary in 1906 and then the General Secretary in 1909. He held this post until 1941. In 1925, Elvin was elected to the General Council of the Trades Union Congress (the TUC) and served as its president in 1938.

Herbert Henry Elvin was also involved in politics. He spent much of the 1920s trying unsuccessfully to be elected as a Labour MP.

Nevertheless, he was able to serve the Labour Party and the political cause as a Trades Unionist. He was an advisor to the International Labour Organisation and served on the executive of the League of Nations Union. The only elected post he managed to secure, other than ones connected with Unions, was as a member of Middlesex County Council. He died on 10th November 1949.

Elvin's roots as a Baptist preacher are shared with many in the Labour movement, once described as owing 'more to Methodism than to Marx'. His concern for those in poverty, which was also seen in his organisation of outings for children from the slums of the East End of London, and his skills in bringing people together have deep roots in his faith.

Olave Baden-Powell

In the first twenty-three years of her life, Olave Soames lived in seventeen different homes. Her father was a brewer, descended from the landed gentry. Olave was born in Wingerworth near Chesterfield on 22nd February 1889. She was educated at home, by her parents and by governesses. In January 1912, on board the ocean liner Arcadian, she met Robert Baden-Powell, already by then famous for his heroism in the Boer war and for founding the Scouting movement. The two shared a birthday, although he was 32 years older than she. In October of that year, they were married in a quiet ceremony in Olave's parish church in Parkstone.

Soon after the Baden-Powells were married, the First World War (1914-1918) began. Olave went to France in 1915, only five months after the birth of her second child, to assist directly in running recreational huts. These huts provided important spaces where service men could relax, find people to talk with, and have a break from the frontline. Olave was involved in serving cocoa, talking with servicemen, and organising musical entertainment. She was ordered home in 1916 because she became ill.

Olave's involvement in scouting and guiding was initially all through her husband. She acted as a secretary for him, and later as his driver. She was a Scout Master for a Boy Scout Troup in Ewhurst, where the Baden-Powells lived at this time. The Girl Guide Movement, begun by Robert and his sister Agnes, had been a response to the demand from girls to join the Scouts. In 1914, Olave was persuaded by Robert to offer her services to the Guides. They turned her down, suggesting she was too young and inexperienced. However, Olave believed that 'when God wants one to do something, He smooths away the difficulties in one's way'. The Girl Guides were reorganised in 1915, and when Olave offered again on her return from France in 1916 her offer was accepted. She became the County Commissioner for Sussex, and at the same time recruited 2840 Guide Commissioners to serve in every county in England. Such was the impression that she made in this role that in October of that year she was unanimously elected as the Chief Commissioner for England. In 1918, her title was changed to Chief Guide. By 1930, she was the World Chief Guide.

As Robert grew more unwell, Olave moved with him to Nyeri in Kenya, and it was there that he died in 1941. This was a huge blow to Olave, who wondered how she could continue. She found the international Guiding and Scouting Movements to be a great consolation and threw herself into work for them. 'I thank God daily', wrote Olave, 'for the wonderful way in which His Divine Hand led us both to come together ... How richly God blessed us both in giving us our work and each other'.

During the Second World War (1939-45), Olave braved the trip home and spent the war organising Guides and Scouts to support the war effort. As soon as the war was over, she toured Europe to encourage the revival of Guiding and Scouting. She had become a global ambassador for Guides and Scouts and would continue in this role for the rest of her life. She visited 111 countries, attending jamborees and supporting Guide and Scout Associations across the world. She led the expansion of the Girl Guide Movement to over six and a half million members worldwide. Her globetrotting only ended when, at the age of 80, her doctor forbade further travel. She died, aged 88, on 25th June 1977. Her ashes were buried in Kenya with her husband.

Olave's faith was deeply important to her. She regarded the Guide and Scout promise to 'do my duty to God' as very important. She was godmother to over 40 children, standing with them and their parents as they were baptised – another duty she took very seriously. In her autobiography, she wrote, 'If I have any message to leave, it is this: Believe in God. He guides and protects you all through life'.

Every 22nd February, the shared birthday of Olave and Robert Baden-Powell, is marked as Thinking Day by the worldwide Girl Guide Movement. On this day, Guides across the world are encouraged to think about their connection with one another, the different cultures they inhabit and the challenges faced by their sister guides. Olave herself wrote of the 'spiritual impact' of Thinking Day: 'these thoughts and prayers are concentrated thus as a live force for the developing of friendship and understanding, for which all peoples are longing'.

Both trades unions and the Girl Guides bring people together for a common cause, understanding that individuals are stronger when they work together. Unions advocate for justice and rights for those who work. The Guides bring greater opportunities for young women. They have grown to become the largest global movement for girls, with currently member organisations in 150 countries and more than 10 million members worldwide. Two central themes were present from the earliest days of the movement: domestic skills and 'a kind of practical feminism which embodies physical fitness, survival skills, camping, citizenship training, and career preparation', with the motto 'Be Prepared' and a promise to do something kind for someone else every day, without reward and without being asked.

Both Herbert Henry Elvin and Olave Baden-Powell understood the importance of bringing people together in fellowship and mutual support, and at the root of why they each did that was a faith in God who also brings people together. Through the movements and organisations that they championed, they enacted their faith and improved the lives of many others.

A Prayer for Pilgrims

God who called a people together,

 we give you thanks for Herbert Henry Elvin

 and Olave Baden-Powell,

 for their work for justice and opportunities for others,

 for their care for those in need,

 and for their skill in organising groups of people.

May we follow in the way of Christ,

 working for friendship and understanding,

 offering our skills and energy to help others,

 and thinking about what brings us together with others.

We pray for the work of Trades Unions and the Girl Guides,

 that they may be sources of justice and friendship

 and bring a voice to those who might not be heard.

We ask this in the name of Jesus,

 who called together women and men

 into a new movement of God's people.

 Amen.

'Together we belong, together we are strong' (Stronger Together
https://www.flashlyrics.com/lyrics/military-wives/stronger-together-77*)*

Where to go

Eckington in north-east Derbyshire has no monument or memorial to Herbert Henry Elvin of which we are aware. He does however have a portrait in the Photographs Collection of the National Portrait Gallery (https://www.npg.org.uk/collections/search/portrait/mw175771)

Chesterfield has done better by Olave Baden-Powell, with a blue plaque marking the site of her childhood home at West House. This is on West Bars, opposite the Post Office, S49 1PF. Her birthplace, at Stubbing Court in Wingerworth, S42 6QY is a private house.

Olave's married surname is also used for Baden Powell Road, S40 2RL in the town, and for the name of a care home, the Baden Powell Centre, S41 7LP.

19. War and Peace:

William Harold Coltman

Winshill, 19th-20th centuries

The most decorated 'other rank' soldier in the First World War was a Christian pacifist, who risked his life to save others. ('Other rank' means he was not a commissioned officer).

William Harold Coltman was born in Rangemore, near Burton upon Trent on 17th November 1891. After school, he worked as a gardener, and he was a member of the Plymouth Brethren. He also taught the Sunday School in Winshill, where he lived. William was a faithful believer, and the Brethren were a largely pacifist church. Nonetheless, he volunteered for the army in the early months of the war, in January 1915. He joined the 1st/6th North Staffords as a rifleman, but was allowed to serve as a stretcher bearer due to his pacifist Christian beliefs.

In this role, Coltman demonstrated quiet bravery on a regular basis. He was mentioned in dispatches on 1st July 1916, for his courage. He also received the French *Croix de Guerre*, awarded for those who distinguish themselves by acts of heroism.

In February 2017, Coltman rescued an officer from no-mans land. The officer was leading a working party on a misty night. The mist cleared, and the party came under fire. The officer was wounded in the thigh and Coltman immediately went out to retrieve him, whilst under heavy shelling. For this, he was awarded the Military Medal (MM). He went on to win a bar to his MM, effectively a second medal, for his bravery and conduct over several days in June 1917. On 6th

June, an ammunition dump was hit by mortar fire. Coltman took command to remove the lights from the dump. The following day, he took the lead in treating men injured when the company headquarters was shelled. About a week later, he rescued men trapped under a collapsed trench tunnel.

The following month, July 1917, Coltman spent a night under shelling and machine gun fire as he searched for injured soldiers. His bravery and conduct on this occasion earned him a Distinguished Conduct Medal (DCM). The citation reads: 'Conspicuous gallantry and devotion to duty in evacuating wounded from the front line at great personal risk under shell fire. His gallant conduct undoubtedly saved many lives, and he continued throughout the night to search for wounded under shell and machine gun fire, and brought several in. His absolute indifference to danger had a most inspiring effect upon the rest of his men'.

William Coltman's medal group including VC, DCM and Bar and MM and Bar, are on display at the Staffordshire Regiment Museum.
(see http://vconline.org.uk/william-h-coltman-vc/4586221531)

At the end of September 1918, Coltman's regiment captured the Riqueval Bridge, a decisive action in the Battle of the St Quentin Canal. Coltman tended the wounded and ensured that none were left behind. He received a bar to his DCM for this. Again, the citation tells the story: 'On the 28th September, 1918, near the St. Quentin Canal, near Bellenglise, he dressed and carried many wounded men under heavy artillery fire. During the advance on the following day he still remained at his work without rest or sleep, attending the wounded, taking no heed of either shell or machine-gun fire, and never resting until he was positive that our sector was clear of wounded. He set the highest example of fearlessness and devotion to duty to those with him'.

Only five days later, Coltman was at Mannequin Hill near Saint-Quentin in northern France. On 3rd October, he heard that wounded men had been left behind in the valley in front of the hill. He returned to find them. The German army still occupied the high ground, and kept up heavy machine gun fire. Coltman went into the fire, time after time, to rescue the injured. He carried each man back, gave him to another stretcher bearer, and then returned to the gunfire to find another. He kept this up for forty-eight hours, before finally resting. For this he was awarded the Victoria Cross (VC), the highest award for bravery that the British army can award. The citation for the medal reads: 'For most conspicuous bravery, initiative and devotion to duty. During the operations at Mannequin Hill, N.E. of Sequehart, on the 3rd and 4th October 1918, Lance Corporal Coltman, a stretcher-bearer, hearing that wounded had been left behind during a retirement, on his own initiative, went forward alone in the face of fierce enfilade fire, found the wounded, dressed them, and on three successive occasions carried comrades on his back to safety, thus saving their lives. This very gallant N.C.O. [Non-Commissioned Officer] tended the wounded unceasingly for forty-eight hours'.

Undoubtedly, Coltman saved many lives during the war. His many awards for bravery show his consistent willingness to put himself in danger to rescue others. But he refused to see himself as anything special. A hero's welcome was prepared for his return at the end of the war. He avoided this, by leaving the train early and walking the final twenty miles home. There was public recognition when he was invested with his Victoria Cross on 22nd May 1919. Again, however, he avoided the civic reception held in his honour. With hindsight, it seems likely that this was a mixture of his personality, combined with a deep Christian humility, and the trauma of witnessing so much death and destruction.

William returned to Winshill. He married Eleanor May Dolman, and worked for the Parks Department as a groundskeeper. During the Second World War, he commanded the Burton Cadet Force from 1943 until 1951. He never sought the limelight. Like many who returned from the war, he rarely spoke about his experiences during that time. Instead, he tended flower beds in Winshill near where he lived, and had a number of allotments. He and Eleanor had two children.

William retired from his work with the Park Department in 1963. On his retirement, a portrait was commissioned. At its unveiling he said 'it is my sincere hope that future generations of this town will know nothing of war except what they read in history books'.

Until he was unable to do so, he continued to meet as a member of the Brethren in Winshill. He died at the age of 82 on 29th June 1974, and was buried in Winshill churchyard, along with his wife. In keeping with his avoidance of celebrity, it is her name that appears first on the gravestone.

William Coltman was a man of enormous courage, who won all his medals without ever firing a shot. His witness to the peace of God, coupled with his refusal to stand by and allow others to suffer make him an inspirational figure. His peaceable nature, as a stretcher bearer and as a gardener, his immense courage, and his humility are all rooted in his faith. His faith also gave him inspiration and comfort which enabled him to bear the trauma that he had witnessed.

A Prayer for Pilgrims

God of peace and of courage,

we give you thanks for William Coltman,

for his commitment to peace,

for his heroism in times of war,

and for his patient tending of gardens.

May we follow in the way of Christ,

with courage to hold to our beliefs,

commitment to helping others,

and gentleness in all we do.

We pray for those fighting in wars today,

that they might have courage to do what is right

and compassion for those who are injured.

We ask this in the name of Jesus,

whose courageous witness to your peace

led him to the place of death.

Amen.

'Shades of War in the Peace Garden'
The illustration shows WW1 stretcher bearers drawn from contemporary
sketches, including one of William Coltman, walking through the Coltman VC
Memorial Peace Wood.

Where to Go

Winshill:

William Coltman's links to Derbyshire are through his connection with Winshill, East Staffordshire, which is within the Diocese of Derby. It was in Winshill that he taught Sunday school, lived, married, raised a family, and gardened. His grave in the churchyard of St Mark's Church, Winshill, DE15 0HS was re-dedicated in 2014, having been restored by the Victoria Cross Trust.

The Coltman VC Memorial Peace Wood was opened as a public place of remembrance on Mill Hill Lane, Winshill, DE15 0AX at the recreation ground he tended. In addition, the wood commemorates the 94 men from the area who did not return from the war. A birch tree has been planted for each of them.

Elsewhere:

William's medals are on display at the Staffordshire Regiment Museum at Whittington, WS14 9PY where there is a replica First World War trench named in his honour.

The headquarters building of Defence Medical Services at Whittington Barracks is named Coltman House.

20. The Repton Archbishops:

William Temple, Geoffrey Fisher and Michael Ramsey

Repton, 20th century

We end back at Repton with more ABCs. This time the abbreviation stands for Archbishop of Canterbury. Three successive Archbishops have had strong links with Repton School: William Temple and Geoffrey Fisher were Headmasters, and Michael Ramsey was a pupil at the school. All three, in different ways, made important contributions to the Church of England in their roles as Archbishop. This school made its mark on them all.

William Temple

William Temple was born on 15th October 1881, in the Bishop's Palace in Exeter, where his father Frederick was the Bishop. Frederick Temple went on to be Bishop of London and then Archbishop of Canterbury.

As a child, William was known to dress up in smaller versions of his father's robes and give sermons to his nursery. He excelled at Rugby school, and went on to study Classics at Balliol College, Oxford, then became a Fellow and Lecturer in Philosophy at Queen's College in Oxford. During his years in Oxford, William gained a reputation as a teacher and a thinker. He had a settled faith in God, but was constantly pushing to discover whether the orthodox account of the faith was correct. In 1906, he applied to be ordained. However, the Bishop of Oxford refused, as Temple admitted that his belief in the doctrines of the virgin birth and the bodily resurrection was 'shaky'. In 1909, Randall Davidson, then the Archbishop Canterbury, decided that Temple's faith was emerging into orthodoxy and took the risk of ordaining him. Within four years, his risk had paid off, with William writing that, 'I believe in the Virgin Birth...it wonderfully holds before the imagination the truth of Our Lord's Deity and so I am glad that it is in the Creed. Similarly I believe in our Lord's Bodily Resurrection'.

In 1910, William Temple was made Headmaster of Repton school. He had his doubts about the appointment, writing to his brother that, 'I doubt if headmastering is really my line'. In this he was probably right. He was known to the boys as 'Billy', hardly a mark of respect. Discipline was not something that came naturally: on learning that some boys had been stealing from the school shop, he appealed to the culprits' sense of honour. His approach was to build personal relationships with the boys in order to inspire them into good behaviour. One of his colleagues wrote of this reticence, 'Of such are saints made, but not headmasters'.

Yet this was an important time for him. He made strong connections to some of the older pupils, sharing the fruits of his own real struggles in faith. His teachings on St John's Gospel, which were eventually published in 1939, were originally part of his teaching to sixth formers at Repton, where he developed a way of communicating the Christian faith to young people which never left him. The Bursar of Repton wrote to Temple's mother in admiration of her son's preaching: 'the boys even stopped coughing - the highest tribute they ever offer!' William Temple's volume of *Repton School Sermons* is demanding of its audience and stands as an example of his refusal to talk down to the students in his care.

William Temple's brief stint as Headmaster of Repton came to an end in 1914. From Repton, he went to be Rector of St James in Piccadilly, and on to be Bishop of Manchester and then Archbishop of York, finding time to write prolifically. Finally, in 1942, with the nation fearing German invasion, he became Archbishop of Canterbury. Appropriately for a wartime Archbishop, he was enthroned on St George's Day.

As Archbishop of Canterbury, William worked with the Chief Rabbi to found the Council of Christians and Jews to combat anti-Semitism, and spoke in the House of Lords in favour of action to prevent the Nazi atrocities against Jews. In March 1943, he spoke in the Lords to say that, 'Jews are being slaughtered at the rate of tens of thousands a day ... We stand at the bar of history, of humanity and of God'. He was in no way a pacifist and did not condemn the allied bombing of cities in Germany, because he believed it was necessary to overthrow the Nazi regime.

William Temple's other great and longest lasting achievements are in the field of ecumenism and in politics. He was one of the early supporters of ecumenism, the bringing together of different Christian churches and denominations. He wrote that, 'I believe in the Holy Catholic Church, and sincerely regret that it does not at present exist'. Both the British Council of Churches and the World Council of Churches count William Temple as one of their founders (even though the latter didn't come into existence until after the war, in 1948). His theological skills and his ability to bring people together made him an effective leader in the ecumenical movement, which he regarded as 'the great new fact of our era'. In bringing together people from across the world and across the different denominations, William Temple made a huge contribution to making it so.

However, in the world of politics, William was more controversial. He joined the Labour Party in 1918 and became the first President of the Workers' Educational Association, which championed the education of working people. At the outbreak of the Second World War, he urged the hearers of a broadcast address to 'look beyond the conflict to the restoration of peace, and dedicate ourselves to the creation of a world-wide order which shall be fair to the generations yet unborn'. In the year he became Archbishop of Canterbury, he published the short book *Christianity and Social Order* which became his best-known book. In it he set out his vision for a post-war society that reflected the dignity of every human being. It is one of the first outlines of the welfare state, and was influential on the Labour government of 1945 which brought in huge reforms.

He brought the churches together to support the Education Act of 1944, which was another source of post-war reform. Yet even this work crossed parties, and later Conservative leaders such as Edward Heath (Prime Minister from 1970-1974) found Temple's work to be an inspiration.

At his last public appearance, at a clergy retreat, he arrived in an ambulance and spoke standing on one foot. William had suffered from gout all of his life – he endured the first attack at the age of two – and this latest bout contributed to his death, on 26th October 1944. He did not see the end of the war, or the implementation of so much of what he had hoped and worked for. He was the first Archbishop to be cremated, and is buried in Canterbury Cathedral.

Geoffrey Fisher

William Temple's successor at Canterbury had also been his successor at Repton School: Geoffrey Fisher. Born on 5th May 1887, in Nuneaton, Fisher was the son, grandson and great-grandson of Rectors of Higham on the Hill in Leicestershire. After school and university, Geoffrey went to teach at Marlborough College, and was ordained. It was from Marlborough that he was recruited to be the Headmaster of Repton.

A young man, only 27 when he arrived at Repton, he approached his task with energy. He needed that energy. Two months after his appointment, the First World War broke out. Six masters and sixty of the older boys signed up to the army. As well as the uncertainty and the fear engendered by the outbreak of war, Geoffrey found that the school needed organisation. Discipline and administration had not been strong qualities in his predecessor, and both came more naturally to Geoffrey. Remembered for being at times fierce, at times merely firm, he imposed the needed authority, reorganised the timetable and curriculum, and improved the facilities.

His sermons in chapel were on practical themes, though he confessed that he had never converted anyone by his preaching. He did, however, care deeply for both the school and its boys. One evening, shortly after the end of the war, he was walking through Repton and spotted a chamber pot perched on top of the market cross in the heart of the village. Not wishing to allow blame to be allotted either to the school or its boys, he climbed the cross to remove it himself. Just as he reached the chamber pot and grasped it firmly in his hand, the local policeman arrived on the scene. A troubling few moments followed as the policeman questioned the headmaster, who he thought had been in the act of putting the pot onto the cross!

In 1932, having been at Repton for eighteen years, Fisher was appointed Bishop of Chester, then Bishop of London in 1939, before once again succeeding William Temple, this time as Archbishop of Canterbury. He was enthroned as Archbishop on 19th April 1945.

Geoffrey Fisher had led the Diocese of London through the devastation of the blitz with courtesy, skill, and determination, and by the time he became Archbishop the war was very nearly over, and victory looked assured. Once again, his capacity for organisation came to the fore as he presided over a renewal of the Canons, the church law, which had not been revised properly since the seventeenth century. This is hardly a project of great excitement, but one that had a huge impact upon the day-to-day smooth running of the Church.

There were, of course, many more events during Geoffrey Fisher's time at Canterbury that are of more interest. He presided at the marriage of Princess Elizabeth, and then crowned her as Queen Elizabeth II. He travelled a great deal, which had not been something that his predecessors had done, which enabled him to bring the churches of the Anglican Communion into a closer relationship, and also to deepen and develop the ecumenical work of his predecessor. He put a great deal of effort into building relationships with the other Protestant churches in England, but he is most remembered as the first Archbishop of Canterbury since the Reformation to meet with the Pope. On 2nd December 1960, he met with Pope John XXIII, who had called the Second Vatican Council the previous year. In doing this, Archbishop Fisher had to stand firm against anti-Catholic prejudice in England and in the Church of England. Some even approached the Queen to ask her to prevent it. However, his perspective was greatly desired, and he is also said to have advised those organising the Vatican Council on how to obtain observers from other churches.

In 1961, shortly after his visit to the Pope, Geoffrey Fisher retired. He was made a life peer, but chose to serve as an assistant priest in a parish in Trent, near Sherborne in Dorset, where he died on 15th September 1972, after a short illness. The Sunday before he died, he was worshipping in the parish church of Trent as usual. The day before his death he suffered a slight stroke, and when his wife came to help him he told her, 'Don't bother me dear, I'm busy dying'.

Geoffrey Fisher rarely tops anyone's lists of favourite or important Archbishops, but as one contemporary put it, 'When Geoffrey was headmaster of Repton, everybody said "What a good school Repton is", but nobody ever said: "What a great headmaster Fisher is!" When he was Bishop of London, everybody said: "How well the diocese is running", but nobody said: "How admirably Fisher is running it!" And it will be the same all his life'. It continues to work in this way.

Michael Ramsey

In 1961, Archbishop Fisher was preparing to retire from Canterbury and Prime Minister Harold Macmillan called him in to discuss his successor. 'Dr Ramsey is a theologian, a scholar and a man of prayer. Therefore, he is entirely unsuitable as Archbishop of Canterbury' was Fisher's advice to Macmillan. Later, Macmillan interviewed Ramsey. 'Fisher doesn't seem to approve of you', he told Ramsey. Ramsey's characteristic response was to defend Fisher. 'Fisher was my headmaster and has known my deficiencies for a long time', he replied. 'Well', replied Macmillan, 'he isn't going to be my headmaster', and offered the job to Ramsey. Later, Macmillan was to say of his choice of Michael Ramsey that 'I thought we had had enough of Martha and it was time for some Mary'. This neatly encapsulates the difference between the two.

Born on 14th November 1904, in Cambridge, Michael Ramsey would become the third Archbishop of Canterbury in succession with a connection to Repton school. His parents were both children of clergy. His father, Arthur, was the son of a Congregationalist minister and taught mathematics at Magdalene College in Cambridge. The family worshipped at a Congregationalist Chapel, Emmanuel, in Cambridge. His mother, Agnes, was the daughter of an Anglican vicar. She was also a socialist and a suffragette, and combined her Christian faith with a committed social conscience. Michael was baptised by his Anglican grandfather in Horbling in Lincolnshire, but never forgot his nonconformist roots. Nor did he forget that his elder brother, Frank, was an atheist.

Michael arrived at Repton School in 1918, under Geoffrey Fisher as headmaster. He was not happy at school. He had never been very well coordinated and although cricket and rugby were important parts of the school's curriculum and identity, Ramsey enjoyed neither. He became known as an eccentric: studious and peculiar. However, he found three masters that he looked back to with gratitude. One was Henry Balmforth, a classics teacher and priest. Another was Mr Burd the librarian, who shared Michael's lack of interest in cricket, and was said to be the only master in the school who didn't know the name of the cricket captain. The third was Mr Hayward, who was a gentle teacher with an interest in moths and butterflies.

Michael was happier in his later years at the school. By then, his biographer suggests, he had 'won the right to be an oddity'. He found the school debating society to be the place he could make his own. He could think on his feet and hold the interest of his peers with his speeches.

Michael came into conflict with the school over the obligation to be part of the Officer Training Corps (OTC). Never a pacifist, he was nevertheless determined that military training was not what he wanted. He had to explain this to headmaster Fisher, and it became something of a contest of wills – one that Michael eventually won. He made Fisher admit that the OTC was not a compulsory part of schooling, and asked his father to write him a letter supporting his dissent. Result: he did not join the Officer Training Corps.

Repton also proved to be a place where Michael explored his faith. In the face of challenging conversations with his elder brother, Michael was forced to examine the truth of his belief. Whilst never losing respect for atheists, he found a firm and robust faith in his latter years at Repton. He also found himself attracted to Anglo-Catholic forms of religious practice, despite his childhood nourishment by a Congregationalist Chapel at home in Cambridge and the Book of

Common Prayer in the Repton Chapel. His move to a more Anglo-Catholic approach to faith, firmly Anglican but prepared to challenge the Protestant establishment, is evidence of his determination and self-belief. Headmaster Fisher wrote in his final report on Ramsey that he was, 'A boy with plenty of force of character who, in spite of certain uncouthnesses, has done good service on his own lines'. The older Ramsey would look back with pride on the way his headmaster pointed to 'his own lines'.

From Repton, Michael Ramsey went on to study classics at his father's college in Cambridge, where he became an impressive speaker at the Cambridge Union, and was once hailed by Asquith as a future leader of the Liberal party. But it was at Cambridge that Ramsey gained clarity that his future lay not in politics but in the church. William Temple, then Bishop of Manchester, led a mission to Cambridge in 1926. Temple's thoughtful approach in connecting with the realities of the world, combined with his skill in engaging with young people, impressed Michael and was the final part of the bridge that took him to ordination.

After his ordination Michael, served as a curate in Liverpool and then went to teach at Lincoln Theological College, where he wrote his first book. In order to accomplish this, he regularly had to leave his room for the student common room below to ask for quiet so that he could write. A rumour grew among the students, no doubt a further product of Ramsey's eccentricity, that he had written the book on the wallpaper of his room! The resulting book, *The Gospel and the Catholic Church* (1936) made his name, and is still read today. From Lincoln he went on to be a Professor of Theology at Durham

University and then at Cambridge University. He wrote more books and taught many students, but through all retained his commitment to being a priest, and in 1952 was made Bishop of Durham. Only four years later, he was elevated to being Archbishop of York, and then in 1961, after his interview with Harold Macmillan, he succeeded Geoffrey Fisher at Canterbury.

As Archbishop of Canterbury, Ramsey presided over the Church of England through the great changes that happened in society during the 1960s. During his tenure, he led the Bishops in the House of Lords to vote for the decriminalisation of homosexuality (1964-5), piloted the Bill to end capital punishment through the Lords (1965), and championed the Race Relations Act (1968). These were controversial positions, but ones that he could see clearly were right and in accordance with Christian faith. He stood firm, despite quite horrific opposition.

Archbishop Ramsey's clarity in seeking the right path over the easy one was also seen abroad. He opposed Ian Smith's refusal to allow Africans to take part in the government of Rhodesia (which became Zimbabwe following Smith's fall). In South Africa, during the vicious apartheid regime which Ramsey described as 'unchristian', he met with Prime Minister Vorster. He later described Vorster as the 'most totally rude man I had ever met'. Again, we can see his strength in the face of opposition.

Within the church, Michael Ramsey also faced controversy. Bishop John Robinson's book *Honest to God* (1963) seemed to many to reject traditional Christian faith. Ramsey's response, a short book called

Image Old and New (1963), was well written but didn't really engage with Robinson's main argument.

He also put much energy into interactions with other churches, working hard at building relationships with Eastern Orthodox churches, and his patient and prayerful theology won him many friends and admirers here. Building on Geoffrey Fisher's meeting with Pope John XXIII, Archbishop Ramsey made a profound personal connection with John XXIII's successor, Pope Paul VI. So strong was this relationship, that after taking part in a service together in Rome, Pope Paul removed his episcopal ring, the sign of his ordination as a bishop, and gave it to Ramsey. In the face of the official Roman Catholic position that Anglican ordinations were 'absolutely null and void', this was a profoundly important gesture. Ramsey continued to wear the ring until his death. Since then, it has been worn by every Archbishop of Canterbury when visiting the Vatican.

However, together with these successes, came a failure. Michael Ramsey had given a great deal of support to a scheme that would have reunited the Church of England and the Methodist Church, but an alliance of the extreme Catholic and Evangelical wings of the Church of England thwarted this. In May 1972, the General Synod (the Church of England's equivalent of parliament) voted 65.81% in favour of the scheme, not quite at the two-thirds majority needed. Archbishop Ramsey was heartbroken, and brought proceedings to an end by quoting the musical Godspell, 'Long Live God'.

Retirement just before his 70th birthday in 1974 took Michael back to former haunts in Durham, York and Oxford. He tried to write theology, but found that it was books on prayer that were produced –

though for him, these two had always been very close. His integration of prayer, ministry, theology and ethics was the enormous gift he gave to the church. He died in Oxford, still wearing Pope Paul VI's episcopal ring, on 23rd April 1988. When asked where he should be buried, he replied, 'I should like to be not far from William Temple'. He was indeed buried near Temple, in the cloister of Canterbury Cathedral.

William Temple, Geoffrey Fisher and Michael Ramsey – three successive Archbishops of Canterbury who all had strong links with Repton School – were very different from one another and brought their varied gifts to both Repton and to the wider Church of England. Temple, the great visionary leader; Fisher, the efficient organiser; and Ramsey, the eccentric man of prayer. All worked for the unity of the church. All worked to serve the people of this country. All worked to make God known in and beyond the church.

A Prayer for Pilgrims

God who leads his people,

    we give you thanks for William Temple,

    Geoffrey Fisher and Michael Ramsey,

    for their vision in times of crisis,

    for their organisation of people,

    and for their prayerfulness and openness to you.

May we follow in the way of Christ,

    seeking the way that leads to the good of all people,

    supporting organisations that bring life and goodness,

    and receiving your gift to be ourselves.

We pray for those who lead your church today,

    that they may be bold in proclaiming the Good News of Jesus,

    and generous in caring for those entrusted to them.

We ask this in the name of Jesus,

    who led many to you through his acts of love.

    Amen.

'Wartime bombing hit London churches severely' from a military archive photo from April 1941 (New Times Paris Bureau Collection)

Where to go

Repton School, DE65 6FH is an integral part of the village of Repton. Access to is limited, due to its nature as a school.

If you can get in to look, the Chapel has a plaque to the three Archbishops (intimidating for any preacher!). Archbishop Fisher left his episcopal robes to the School, and they are displayed in a glass case in one of the school's staff rooms.

The market cross, from which Fisher removed the chamber pot, is more accessible, standing on the main road through the village.

Elsewhere:

Portraits of the three are listed in the National Portrait Gallery Photographs collections: search at https://www.npg.org.uk/collections/about/photographs-collection

21. All Saints and All Souls of Derbyshire

As we end this tour of the Saints of Derbyshire, let us take you to the Cathedral Church of Derby and Derbyshire. Derby Cathedral is, appropriately for this book, dedicated to All Saints – all those, known and unknown, who have followed in the way of Jesus. There are two stained glass windows in Derby Cathedral which were designed by the Welsh artist Ceri Richards. These windows, pictured on the front and back of this book, are not just striking abstract pieces of art that give character and interest to the Cathedral, though they are at least that. They are also important theological statements, and ones that can particularly help our reflections on the saints of Derbyshire.

The All Saints' window properly reflects the grandeur of the 'great cloud of witnesses' (Hebrews 12.1), the people whose faith in God and in Jesus brings them into communion with us. Its bright gold colours show the triumph of the light, the victory of God's purposes. It is almost a picture of the last pieces being put into place, as gradually the building blocks take their rightful places. This is a bright and well-ordered image.

The All Saints' window shows the whole of creation restored and renewed by God. The fact that it is named All Saints tells us that this work of God in restoring and renewing all things comes through the lives of God's people. God is at work in his people, restoring them and through them restoring all creation. At the heart of the window there is a cross, through which all the pieces of creation are woven back together. It is the cross, working in the lives of all the saints, that brings about this renewal and restoration. In the All Saints' window, we see the whole of God's plan being put into effect.

But now turn your attention to the All Souls' window. This is a much darker piece. The sombre hues are broken by flashes of light, but not as yet overcome by them. There is less of the soaring upward movement, somehow the forms are straining against each other. All is in flux, unstable, moving. This is not an ending, but a depiction of the in-between stage. There is struggle here. The light shines in the darkness but has not yet overcome it. If the All Saints' window shows us the victory of God and the restoration of creation, the All Souls' window shows us the struggle to see the light in the midst of darkness, and the messiness in which we now live. This is where we are now. The darkness is very dark, and we all have times when we feel or have felt that darkness.

But even here, the darkness has not won. The darkness is not the focus of the window. The great bright overarching flashes of light draw our eye and hold our attention. The All Souls' window recognises that in the darkness of the present, it is the light of those souls who have loved us, have given of themselves, and have worked for the good of others, that brings light to us. The darkness is darker in this window, but the light seems brighter. The vision of All Saints is shown to us in fleeting glimpses and in partial flashes, by the lives of the holy souls who wait for the day of resurrection when all will be made new. The lives of the Derbyshire Saints make sense only in the hope of the brighter vision of All Saints. Their lives are the flashes of light and hope that help us in the darkness depicted in the All Souls' window.

This book has gathered some of the saints of Derbyshire and tried to tell their stories. In doing that, it has also shone reflected light onto the places in the county where they lived and the history which shaped them. But those mentioned in these pages are not the only saints of Derbyshire, there are many more. Most are the faithful people whose lives were unremarked upon, but who lived out their faith and touched the lives of many. Nor are they all in the past. There are saints of God, great and small, among us today. There always will be.

Christians live under the vision of All Saints, the vision of all creation renewed and restored. But we stand in a place that can still be very dark. And we give thanks. We give thanks for those who bring light into the darkness of our lives. We give thanks for those who gave us love, care, time, energy, guidance and so much more. We give thanks for those who taught us the faith, forgave us our wrongs and picked us up when we had fallen. We give thanks for those whose love enabled our love, whose care drew out our compassion and whose time gave us space to grow and learn to become who we are. Thanks be to God for all the Saints of Derbyshire.

Appendix One: Feast Days

Saints are usually, but not always, remembered on the day that they died. Those dates marked with * are our suggestions for saints who have no recognised feast day. We have usually followed the convention of making these the date of death, but where that is unknown (or where there is a pressing reason to suggest another date) we have used a date that seems appropriate. One saint is, we hope with reason, remembered on Buy a Priest a Beer Day!

Feast Days by Date

13th January*	Joseph Strutt, social reformer and philanthropist, 1844
26th January*	Joseph Hollingworth of Dale Abbey, Methodist preacher, 1836
3rd February	Werburgh, Princess of Mercia, First Abbess of Repton, 699
11th February*	John Whitehurst of Derby, Clockmaker, Geologist and Church Warden of All Saints, Derby, 1788
13th February	Ermenilda, Queen of Mercia, Abbess, Protector of children, c.675
22nd February*	Olave Baden-Powell of Wingerworth and Chesterfield, World Chief Guide, 1977
7th March*	William Ward of Derby and Serampore, Missionary to India, 1823
9th March*	John Gratton of Monyash, Quaker Preacher, 1711/2
19th March	Alkmund, Prince of Northumberland, Martyr, Patron of Derby, 800

24 March*	Thomas Gisborne, Priest, Abolitionist and member of the Clapham Sect, 1846
10th April*	Aelfritha, Abbess of Repton c.697
11th April	Guthlac, Prince of Mercia, Hermit, 714
18th April*	Erasmus Darwin, Doctor, Botanist, poet and abolitionist, 1802
23rd April*	Michael Ramsey, Pupil at Repton, Archbishop of Canterbury, 1988
7th May*	Jedediah Strutt, inventor, industrialist and philanthropist, 1797
16th May*	Cornelius of Depedale (Dale Abbey), Hermit, c.1150.
1st June	Wystan, Prince of Mercia, Martyr, 840
23rd June*	Margaret Lyman of Fritchley, Quaker Preacher c.1682
29th June*	William Harold Coltman of Winshill, Pacifist, most decorated soldier of WWI, gardener, 1974
6th July*	John Hieron, Puritan and Preacher, 1682
8th July*	Thomas Fanshawe Middleton of Kedleston, First Bishop of Calcutta, 1822
18th July	Edburga, Abbess of Repton, c.700
24th July	Nicholas Garlick, Robert Ludlum and Richard Simpson (the Padley Martyrs), Catholic Martyrs of the Reformation, 1558
1st August	Joan Waste, Protestant Martyr of the Reformation, 1556
13th August	Florence Nightingale of Lea, Nurse, Statistician, Social Reformer, 1910
20th August	Catherine Booth of Ashbourne, Founder of the Salvation Army, 1890

21st August	Hardulph, Hermit at Ingleby, 7th C
24th August*	Joseph Wright of Derby, Artist 1797
30th August*	The Village of Eyam, Plague village, 1665-1666
8th September*	Adda and Betti, Evangelists of Derbyshire, c.653
9th September	Bertram, Prince of Mercia, Hermit, 8th C
9th September*	Francis Brown of Mugginton, Repentant Alcoholic, 1723
15th September*	Geoffrey Fisher, Headmaster of Repton, Archbishop of Canterbury, 1972
1st October	Christopher Buxton of Tideswell, Catholic Martyr of the Reformation, 1588
1st October	Edward James of Breaston, Catholic Martyr of the Reformation, 1588
5th October	William Hartley of Wyn, Catholic Martyr of the Reformation, 1588
10th October*	Maria Jacson, Botanist, 1829
26th October	Cedd, Evangelist of Derbyshire, 664
29th October	Modwen, Abbess of Burton, Pilgrim to Rome, Foundress of St Peter's Stapenhill, 7th C
6th November	William Temple, Headmaster of Repton, Archbishop of Canterbury, 1944
10th November	Herbert Henry Elvin of Eckington, Lay Preacher and Trades Unionist, 1949
1st December	Ralph Sherwin of Rodsley, Catholic Martyr of the Reformation, 1581
7th September	Diuma, Evangelist of Derbyshire, First Bishop of Repton, c.658
9th December*	William Strutt, civil engineer and architect, 1830

23rd December*   The Cratcliffe Hermits, 14th C – 16th C

31st December*   John Flamsteed of Denby, First Astronomer Royal, 1719

Feast Days by Saint

Adda	8th September*
Aelfritha	10th April*
Alkmund	19th March
Baden-Powell, Olave	22nd February*
Bertram	9th September
Betti	8th September*
Booth, Catherine	20th August
Brown, Francis	9th September*
Buxton, Christopher	1st October
Cedd	26th October
Coltman, William Harold	29th June*
Cornelius of Depedale	16th May*
Cratcliffe Hermits	23rd December*
Darwin, Erasmus	18th April*
Diuma	7th December
Edburga	18th July
Elvin, Herbert Henry	10th November*
Ermenilda	13th February
Eyam (village of)	30th August*
Fisher, Geoffrey	15th September*

Flamsteed, John	31st December*
Garlick, Nicholas	24th July
Gisborne, Thomas	24th March*
Gratton, John	9th March*
Guthlac	11th April
Hardulph	21st August
Hartley, William	5th October
Hieron, John	6th July*
Hollingworth, Joseph	26th January*
Jacson, Maria	10th October*
James, Edward	1st October
Ludlum, Robert	24th July
Lyman, Margaret	23rd June*
Middleton, Thomas Fanshawe	8th July*
Modwen	29th October
Nightingale, Florence	13th August
Ramsey, Michael	23rd April*
Sherwin, Ralph	1st December
Simpson, Richard	24th July
Strutt, Jedediah	7th May*
Strutt, Joseph	13th January*
Strutt, William	9th December*
Temple, William	6th November
Ward, William	7th March*

Waste, Joan	1st August
Werburgh	3rd February
Whitehurst, John	11th February*
Wright, Joseph	24th August*
Wystan	1st June

Appendix Two: Places connected with the saints

An alphabetical list of the places to go in search of the Derbyshire Saints, and which saints to look for there.

Ashbourne	Erasmus Darwin (Ch. 12)
	John Hieron (Ch. 13)
	Catherine Booth (Ch. 17)
Belper: Chapel & Cottage, Field Row	Strutt Family (Ch. 14)
Belper: Christ Church	Strutt Family (Ch. 14)
Belper: Memorial Gardens	Strutt Family (Ch.14)
Belper: North Mill	Jedediah and William Strutt (Ch. 14)
Belper: River Gardens	Strutt Family (Ch.14)
Birchover	Joan Waste (Ch. 07)
Bonsall	John Gratton (Ch. 08)
Breadsall	Erasmus Darwin (Ch. 12)
	John Hieron (Ch. 13)
Bretby	John Hieron (Ch. 13)
Breedon on the Hill	Hardulph (Ch. 03)
Burton	Modwen (Ch. 03)
Charlesworth	Libby Lane (Foreword)
Chatsworth House	Grotto (Ch. 06)
Chesterfield	Erasmus Darwin (Ch. 12)
	Olave Baden-Powell (Ch. 18)
Cratcliffe	Cratcliffe Hermits (Ch. 06)
Crich	Margaret Lyman (Ch. 08)

Cromford: Heritage Site	Jedediah Strutt (Ch.14)
Dale Abbey	Cornelius of Depedale (Ch. 06)
	John Hieron (Ch. 13)
	Joseph Hollingworth (Ch. 13)
Denby	John Flamsteed (Ch. 10)
Derby Arboretum	Joseph Strutt (Ch.14)
Derby: Bridge Gate	Thomas Gisborne (Ch. 12)
Derby: Cathedral Church of All Saints	Alkmund (Ch. 04)
	Joan Waste (Ch. 07)
	John Whitehurst (Ch. 12)
	Erasmus Darwin (Ch. 12)
	Joseph Wright (Ch. 12)
	Florence Nightingale (Ch. 16)
	All Saints and All Souls (Ch. 21)
Derby: Central Library	Erasmus Darwin (Ch. 12)
Derby: Chapel of St Mary on the Bridge	Padley Martyrs (Ch. 07)
Derby: Council House	Joseph Strutt (Ch. 14)
Derby: Exeter Bridge	Erasmus Darwin (Ch. 12)
Derby: Friargate	Jedediah &William Strutt (Ch. 14)
Derby: Friends Meeting House, St Helen's Street	George Fox (Ch. 08)
Derby: Full Street	Erasmus Darwin (Ch. 12)
Derby: Irongate	Joseph Wright (Ch. 12)
	William Ward (Ch. 15)
Derby: King Street	Thomas Gisborne (Ch. 12)
	Joseph Hollingworth (Ch. 13)
	William Strutt (Ch. 14)

Derby: London Road	Florence Nightingale (Ch. 16)
Derby: Made in Derby Walk of Fame	John Flamsteed (Ch. 10) Joseph Wright (Ch. 12) Florence Nightingale (Ch. 16)
Derby: Museum & Art Gallery	Alkmund (Ch. 04) Erasmus Darwin (Ch. 12) Joseph Wright (Ch. 12) Jedediah Strutt (Ch.14)
Derby: Museum of Making	John Flamsteed (Ch. 10) Erasmus Darwin (Ch. 12) Joseph Wright (Ch. 12) Jedediah Strutt (Ch.14)
Derby: Quad	John Whitehurst (Ch. 12)
Derby: Queens Street	John Flamsteed (Ch. 10) John Whitehurst (Ch. 12) Joseph Wright (Ch. 12)
Derby: St Alkmund's Church	Alkmund (Ch. 04)
Derby: St Alkmund's Well	Alkmund (Ch. 04)
Derby: St Joseph's Church	Joan Waste (Ch. 07) Ralph Sherwin (Ch. 7)
Derby: St Mary's Church	Ralph Sherwin (Ch. 07) Padley Martyrs (Ch. 07) Christopher Buxton (Ch. 07)
Derby: St Peter's Street	Jedediah Strutt (Ch. 14) Joseph Strutt (Ch. 14) Florence Nightingale (Ch. 16)
Derby: St Peter's Church	Thomas Fanshawe Middleton (Ch. 15) William Ward (Ch. 15) Florence Nightingale (Ch. 16)

Derby: St Peter's Churchyard	John Flamsteed (Ch. 10)
Duffield	Alkmund (Ch. 04)
Eckington	Herbert Henry Elvin (Ch. 18)
Egginton	John Hieron (Ch. 13)
Eyam	The villagers of Eyam (Ch. 9)
Findern	Jedediah Strutt (Ch. 14)
Foremark	Viking Repton (Ch. 02) Hardulph (Ch. 03)
Fritchley	Margaret Lyman (Ch. 08)
Hulland Ward	Francis Brown (Ch. 11)
Ilam	Bertram (Ch. 05)
Ingleby	Hardulph (Ch. 03)
Kedleston	Hermitage (Ch. 06) Thomas Fanshawe Middleton (Ch. 15)
Lea	Florence Nightingale (Ch. 16)
Longford	Ralph Sherwin (Ch. 07)
Matlock	John Gratton (Ch. 08) John Whitehurst (Ch. 12)
Milford: Holy Trinity Church	Strutt Family (Ch. 14)
Milford: Hopping Mill Weir	Strutt Family (Ch. 14)
Milford: Milford Bridge	Strutt Family (Ch. 14)
Milford: Moscow Farm	Strutt Family (Ch. 14)
Milford: Schools	Strutt Family (Ch. 14)
Monyash	John Gratton (Ch. 08)
Mugginton	Francis Brown (Ch. 11)

Newton Solney	John Hieron (Ch. 13)
Padley	Padley Martyrs (Ch. 07)
Radbourne	Erasmus Darwin (Ch. 12)
Rodsley	Ralph Sherwin (Ch. 07)
Repton	Aelfritha (Ch. 02) Diuma (Ch. 02) Ermenilda (Ch. 02) Edburga (Ch. 02) Guthlac (Ch. 02) Werburgh (Ch. 02) Wystan (Ch. 02) William Temple (Ch. 20) Geoffrey Fisher (Ch. 20) Michael Ramsey (Ch. 20)
Somersal Herbert	Maria Jacson (Ch. 12)
South Normanton	Jedediah Strutt (Ch.14)
Stapenhill	Modwen (Ch. 03) John Hieron (Ch. 13)
Tideswell	Nicholas Garlick (Ch. 07) Christopher Buxton (Ch. 07)
Trent Washlands	Modwen (Ch. 03)
Wingerworth	Olave Baden-Powell (Ch. 18)
Winshill	William Harold Coltman (Ch. 19)
Wirksworth	Adda (Ch. 01) Betti (Ch. 01) Cedd (Ch. 01) Diuma (Ch. 01)

Acknowledgments

We are grateful to many people for their help and encouragement in bringing this book together. Any errors remain our own.

In particular we would like to thank:

- Bishop Libby Lane for her Foreword.

- Dean Peter Robinson, Carol Thomas, Canon Elizabeth Thomson, and all at Derby Cathedral for encouragement, support and for publishing.

- Christopher Cunliffe, Mary and Christopher Edwards, Paul Elliot, Jane Legh, Jennifer LewisSmith, Michael McNaught, Neil Roberts, Peter Robinson, James Simister, Jacky Taylor and David Truby for proof reading and saving us from some of our mistakes.

- Jacky, Samuel and Ruth Taylor for being dragged to various places to explore saints.

- All Jo's friends who wittingly or unwittingly helped add source material for her illustrations by driving her to out of the way places while she got to know the county: Dave and Heather Gardner, Robert Hubble, Victoria Nailor, Gwen Schaffer and Anthony Till.

- Green Door Studio for facilities and Pandora Johnson for advice on preparation of the linocut illustrations.

- Len Harrow and Chris Day for advice on publishing and the team at John E Wright for guidance through the printing processes.

- Clergy and congregations at Derby Cathedral, the Chapel of St Mary on the Bridge, St Peter's in the City, Breadsall, Tideswell, Repton School, Newton Solney, Wirksworth, Ashbourne, Winshill, Belper and other places for invitations to preach and patience with questions.

- Those who attended workshops at the Diocese of Derby Clergy Conference, and the Mothers Union at Derby Cathedral and in Aston on Trent for their interest and feedback.

- Successive generations of curates in the Diocese of Derby, who humoured Simon's interest in saints around the county.

- Staff at the Manuscripts and Special Collections of the University of Nottingham.

- Derby City Deanery for encouragement, patience, and an enormous capacity for laughter.

All proceeds from this book will support the mission and ministry of Derby Cathedral.

About the Authors

Simon J Taylor

After a short career as a university lecturer, Simon was ordained and spent ten years as a parish priest in Bristol. In 2012 he was installed as Canon Chancellor at Derby Cathedral, and alongside that role he served the Diocese of Derby variously as Continuing Ministry Development Officer, Director of Curate Training, and Area Dean of Derby City Deanery. During his time in Derbyshire, Simon travelled around the county, for work and for pleasure, and walked the Peak Pilgrimage. It was on a visit to Repton that he began to collect the stories of Derbyshire Saints

In 2019 Simon returned to Bristol where he now serves as Director of Ministry Development. Even in Bristol, Simon discovered more Derbyshire Saints!

Simon has published three books: *How to Read the Bible (without switching off your brain)* (SPCK, 2015); *Imitation and Scapegoats* (Grove, 2016); and *"For Just Such a Time as This": Learning from the Book of Esther for Ministry in Difficult Times* (Grove, 2021).